Y/DA

WA 1178258 7

D0490996

£4

UNIVERSITY OF GLAMORGAN
LEARNING RESOURCES CENTRE

Pontypridd,

A New World for Women

Sheila Rowbotham

A New World for Women
Stella Browne: Socialist Feminist

Pluto ⚶ Press

Learning Resources
Centre

First published 1977 by Pluto Press Limited,
Unit 10 Spencer Court, 7 Chalcot Road, London NW1 8LH
Copyright © Pluto Press 1977
ISBN 0 904383 54 7 paperback
    0 904383 55 5 hardback
Cover designed by Richard Hollis, GrR
Frontispiece photograph of Stella Browne in 1937 courtesy of
Keith Hindell
Extracts from 'The Right to Abortion' reprinted by permission of
George Allen & Unwin Limited
Printed in Great Britain by The Camelot Press Limited,
Southampton. 1782587

Contents

Introduction

I became interested in Stella Browne while writing *Hidden from History*. She fought for contraception and abortion as a feminist committed to sexual liberation. She asserted women's control over their own bodies against men's power of sexual ownership but understood that this was only one aspect of a more general social and economic struggle for liberation. She fought as a socialist as well as a feminist. Her insistence on sexual self-determination and her personal intransigence meant she was as often at odds with her allies as with her enemies. Her socialism and her feminism involved her in a continuing double struggle. It also made her search for connections which have been raised again by the contemporary women's movement. She tried to relate the specific oppression of women as a sex to the emancipation of the working class. Recognising that changes in the ownership and control of production were not enough for women, she saw there had to be a transformation in the circumstances of reproduction so that women could choose or refuse maternity without that economic and social dependence on the man within the family which exists in capitalism. This had to be accompanied by profound inner changes in sexual relationships and in men and women's feeling about sex and love. Although she did not analyse biological reproduction and the domestic labour of women together, as essential to capitalism as the exploitation of the waged labour force, she was aware of the political significance of sexual control.

The socialist movement has never been able to come to terms with the struggle around reproduction which is not only crucial for the liberation of women but a means of extending revolutionary transformation into all aspects of everyday life. So I wondered whether there had been other women like her and how she arrived at her ideas. I wondered what had been the impact upon socialists and upon the labour movement of the campaign for birth control in which she was so deeply involved.

I began to find out more about her for a talk at the Marx Memorial Library in the autumn of 1973 and I am grateful to Keith Hindell who gave me information and references for this. The growth of the National Abortion Campaign gave her ideas an immediate relevance and I travelled the country talking about Stella Browne and birth control and abortion between the wars. I have encountered on these travels a few modern versions of her old opponents. There is still the odd marxist lurking in meetings ready to argue that birth control, abortion, sexual pleasure and women's liberation are all diversions. Fortunately they are an increasingly rare species. A more serious problem is the recent attempt to restrict even the limited right to abortion which women gained from the 1967 Act. Moreover the crisis in the health service endangers all the laboriously won reforms of birth control and maternity provision as well as abortion. The old battles have to be fought again.

Questions, comments and criticisms at these meetings helped to shape *A New World for Women*, and more general discussions in the women's movement about reproduction have helped me to think about Stella Browne's ideas. I have also been made increasingly aware of how little is known about the general involvement of women in political organisations. Though I had to focus, for reasons of space and time, on the birth control campaign in the 'twenties and its impact on the left, it became more and more evident that there are much wider mysteries about the whole context of sexual debate in the history of the socialist movement and that the actual relationship of both women's organisations to male-dominated political parties and of personal relations between the sexes in left groups never seemed to get into history. When I read general histories of the Labour Party or the Communist Party – including ones written since the emergence of the women's liberation movement – it was as if socialists between the wars had existed outside any experience of the family and had never thought or argued about relations between the sexes. I knew that this certainly was not the case. I became more suspicious. If the bits I knew about did not fit, perhaps there was somewhere a different jigsaw picture altogether.

I am afraid I've only filled in a corner and the rest is up to you. Fortunately it is all still near enough to belong to memory if not to history. Two comments which Zelda Curtis and Daphne Morgan made in meetings about Stella Browne have left me convinced that accounts of what was discussed and done at the branch level of politics would be one way of illuminating this missed-out history. Zelda Curtis described sitting round reading Havelock Ellis in a Communist Party branch in the 1930s and Daphne Morgan said that when she joined the Battersea CP in the mid-thirties the secretary whisked her, with other new women recruits, off to the local birth control clinic, getting her fitted with a diaphragm and onto the clinic committee.

Dora Russell's memories of the birth control campaign

in the 'twenties have both helped and inspired me. Her letters and conversations have given me not only information but a glimpse of what it felt like to be a socialist and a feminist between the two world wars. This recognition of a lost sisterhood has been all the more valuable as part of the recovery of a broken and buried political tradition. It gives you great confidence in the world to know that you did not sprout out of nowhere.

There is also the beginnings of a feminist history which is making it possible to think about our past quite differently, and a growing interest in the history of sexual politics in relation to socialism. I have found particular reassurance in writing about Stella Browne and the struggle for control over the reproduction of life from Barbara Taylor's research on the Owenite socialist feminists' views about marriage and the family; Angus McLaren and Linda Gordon's writing on birth control and abortion in the nineteenth and early twentieth centuries; Jane Lewis's articles, published and unpublished on the new feminism, birth control and family allowances; and the Political Economy of Women Group's work on the state and reproduction.

I am also grateful to Sue Bruley, Bob Cant, Val Clarke, Sue Sharpe, Jeff Weeks and David Widgery who read and commented on the manuscript, to Juliet Ash and Ann Scott who answered queries on abortion and birth control, to Jenny Morris for the Index, and again to Val Clarke for typing.

December 1976

Section 1
Stella Browne: Socialist and Feminist

Early in 1912 a controversy erupted in the letter pages of the feminist paper *The Freewoman* on the question of female sexuality. Kathlyn Oliver, a feminist who had been involved in the organisation of domestic servants, wrote criticising the magazine's commitment to 'the new morality'. 'How can we possibly be Freewomen if, like the majority of men, we become the slaves of our lower appetites.'

Kathlyn Oliver said she was unmarried, nearly thirty, had 'always practised abstinence'[1] and was in the best of health. This provoked a letter signed 'New Subscriber', protesting against the denial of female sexuality and quoting Havelock Ellis's work on 'auto-erotism'.

'How many single women have entirely refrained from these practices?'[2] asked 'New Subscriber'. The correspondence continued with Kathlyn Oliver maintaining that chastity did not affect women adversely, that sex appeared repulsive to women without love and that 'New Subscriber' must be 'of the male persuasion'.[3] 'New Subscriber' asserted that women should live as they wanted but resisted the attempt to impose abstinence on women.[4] In July 'New Subscriber' came out as Stella Browne.[5]

Stella Browne was then in her early thirties. She was born in Canada and educated on the continent and at

Somerville College Oxford. She worked as a librarian at Morley College in South London[6] and translated various German works including Van de Velde's *Ideal Marriage*, and *The Diary of Otto Braun* which was introduced by Havelock Ellis.

Already in 1912 she was associated with sexual radical causes supporting the Divorce Law Reform Union.[7] In 1914 she became involved in a campaign organised by the Malthusian League in South London to inform workers of contraceptive methods.[8] She worked with Dr Binnie Dunlop, a member of the League in Southwark. Stella Browne was to continue working for birth control in the Malthusian League (later the New Generation League) throughout the 1920s. In 1936 she was one of the founder members of the Abortion Law Reform Association. She was a feminist who asserted women's right to sexual pleasure against the tendency of some feminists like Kathlyn Oliver who saw sex as a male imposition from which women should be freed. She was also a socialist working first in the Communist Party and then in the Labour Party.

She argued against the suspicion among some marxists of birth control as a palliative which would divert workers from revolution, as well as the desire of reformist labour leaders to defend the family and exclude sexual questions from politics. She was always a minority even within causes supported by minorities, battling all her life for connections between movements, a permanent oppositionist, distrusted as an extremist by more cautious reformers. Dora Russell, who was also a campaigner for birth control in the 1920s and, like Stella Browne, a socialist feminist, remembers Browne as:

what we used to call a war-horse, a sort of militant suffrage type, rather untidy, careless about her looks and appearance. Quite irrepressible at getting-up and interrupting a meeting or asking questions.[9]

Where did the war-horse get her politics from? Stella
Browne's sexual radicalism owed much to Havelock Ellis's
writing on the psychology of sex. She appears to have known
Ellis by 1914[10] and had read his works by 1912 when she
became involved in the dispute in *The Freewoman*. In 1915
she gave a paper on 'The Sexual Variety and Variability
among Women and their Bearing upon Social Reconstruction', quoting Ellis and Housman in support of her
arguments. She also mentioned the work of Dr C.V.Drysdale,
a member of the Malthusian League, which had campaigned
since the nineteenth century for population control, and
Margaret Sanger,[11] the American birth controller she had met
with the Drysdales and Binnie Dunlop towards the end of
1914. Sanger is particularly significant because the
connections she was making and the influences upon her were
very close to Browne's.

Margaret Sanger and her husband were then combating
the Comstock Law which made it illegal to send
contraceptive information through the post. Sanger's *The
Woman Rebel* was seized on the grounds of obscenity before
she went to Europe. While she was away *Family Limitation*,
her pamphlet on birth control printed by a member of the
revolutionary syndicalist IWW, was distributed partly by the
IWW and members of the Socialist Party. Sanger went to
Europe apparently unaware of the nineteenth-century
tradition of sexual radicalism in the United States.

Contraceptive techniques and free unions had been not
only discussed but practised in some of the early utopian
communities. Owen's son Robert Dale Owen published his
Moral Physiology in 1830 in America and another work on
birth control, Charles Knowlton's *Fruits of Philosophy*

appeared two years later. Sexual radicalism persisted within free thought in the 1870s. Ezra Heywood, for example, asserted 'the natural right and necessity of Sexual Self Government' in his essay *Cupids Yokes*.[12] The anarchist Emma Goldman who moved in the same circles as Margaret Sanger in New York was an important connection with this nineteenth-century sexual radicalism.

However, Sanger embarked on a more roundabout journey, going to Britain in the hope of meeting Edward Carpenter, a friend of Ellis and author of *Love's Coming of Age*. Encouraged by the IWW member Big Bill Haywood she also went to France to learn about contraception from revolutionary syndicalists.[13] In fact Emma Goldman had already attended the first birth control conference in Paris in 1900 with the French syndicalist Victor Dave and the English neo-Malthusians the Drysdales.[14] Carpenter and Ellis were also both aware of the American free love tradition.

An important aspect of the utopian communitarian attempt to change sexual relations was the search for perfection. Accordingly they did not always favour contraception but emphasised the need to transform sexuality itself. At the Oneida community in the last quarter of the century, for example, a system of complex marriage replaced monogamy. Births were regulated by the men holding back their orgasms, possibly by diverting sperm into the urethra. This form of birth control was called 'male continence' by its discoverer J.H.Noyes. It was taken a stage further by Alice B.Stockham, author of *Karezza* in 1896. Stockham advocated soul unions – prolonged intercourse without orgasm for both men and women. Behind these ideas was the search for greater control over the body and ultimately for more direct relations between the sexes, when contraception was both awkward and unreliable.

The pursuit of perfection in intercourse was seen as a vital means of extending human control into areas of experience which were usually regarded as natural or instinctive.[15]

Carpenter was dubious about the existing methods of contraception and quoted Stockham approvingly in *Love's Coming of Age*. He saw the theoretical significance of separating erotic pleasure from procreation but this did not initially imply birth control.[16] He was eventually to be convinced by Marie Stopes. Ellis was attracted by the perfectionists' vision of sexual mystical communion but unlike many American sexual radicals he did not connect this to a more general transformation of all social relations. He was more interested in the early eugenic experiments at Oneida as a solution to problems in society.

On this visit to Europe Sanger was to be greatly influenced by Havelock Ellis who persuaded her that birth control should be disassociated from her revolutionary connections with the IWW. He sent her to Holland where she met Dr Rutgers who ran an early birth control clinic. Rutgers opposed her support of women teaching one another and convinced her that birth control advice should be given by doctors. Through Ellis she read about the radical history of birth control in the early nineteenth century, studied works by Annie Besant, George Drysdale and learned of John Humphrey Noyes's sexual and eugenic experimenting at Oneida. Among the pamphlets she wrote while in England was *Magnetation Methods of Birth Control* in which she described amplexus reservatus, the Oneida technique.[17]

Margaret Sanger and Stella Browne, both socialists and feminists committed to sexual liberation, had much in common. Sanger must have been able to tell Stella Browne about the contemporary American movement, her paper *The*

Woman Rebel, and her pamphlet *Family Limitation*. Stella Browne wrote to her American friend in Paris just when William Sanger's imprisonment on a Comstock obscenity charge forced Marget Sanger's return to America.[18]

I simply won't believe that I shall never see you again. We are going to meet again someday and in the meanwhile I'll do what I can, though it won't be as much as I should like to do. . . . It has been one of the *biggest* and one of the *dearest* things in my life to have met and known you.[19]

They stayed in contact, Stella Browne telling Sanger of the doings of the Society for Sex Psychology, of hopes for sex education, circulating Sanger's *Birth Control Review*, sending news of Havelock Ellis, Edward Carpenter and Laurence Housman and hailing the Russian Revolution.[20] In 1920 when Margaret Sanger visited England again, propagandising for birth control, Stella Browne was at the public meeting held by the Malthusian League in Caxton Hall to welcome her.[21]

Sanger also became friendly with Rose Witcop, an anarchist who believed in women's liberation. Rose Witcop came from the Jewish East End anarchist movement and wrote for the feminist paper *The Freewoman* in 1912.[22] She lived in a free union with Guy Aldred, a revolutionary socialist, whose politics were influenced by Marx, Bakunin and revolutionary syndicalism. Aldred consciously associated himself with a radical sexual tradition which he traced from the utopian socialists through free thought. He became a supporter of birth control on the grounds of the right to knowledge. In 1907 he had published one of his speeches 'The Religion and Economics of Sex Oppression' in which he opposed Malthus and advocated celibacy as a means of birth control – a view he later revised.[23]

Margaret Sanger stayed with Witcop and Aldred on this visit. Like Stella Browne, Rose Witcop became a passionate advocate of birth control. Indeed Aldred says Rose Witcop became more involved in birth control agitation than in anarchism.[24] Sanger's early political connections had been with socialists, anarchists and syndicalists. Emma Goldman certainly influenced her. She took over tactics of direct action, defying the law on birth control and then campaigning round the consequences. Rose Witcop approached the question of birth control in a similar way. But already by the end of the First World War Margaret Sanger was moving towards the right, hoping to win more conservative support for birth control as a single issue.[25] However, before and during the First World War she was part of a minority within the left advocating birth control. Sanger's feminism made her insist on the woman's right to control her own body rather than the right to knowledge or birth control as a cure for poverty. But she did not pursue the connection between control over procreation and control over production.

Stella Browne was remarkable in *not* isolating birth control but in continuing to make connections between sexual politics and socialism in the 1920s and '30s. Although she had contact with the older British free thought and sexual radicalism of the late nineteenth century, with Besant and Bradlaugh through the Malthusian League, and with Carpenter and Ellis, she was working in a quite different social and political setting in the period immediately before and after the First World War. This was partly because technical improvements in contraception made ideas of the separation of sexual pleasure from procreation more realistic. In Holland, for example, Dr Rutgers' clinic provided women with the Mensinga diaphragm or dutch cap which was a significant improvement on the Mizpah cervical pessary. The technical means of securing Sanger's demand that women should control their own sexuality was thus available. There was also a growing movement linking feminism, homosexual liberation and socialism in Europe, particularly in Germany. The example of the Russian Revolution, where Alexandra Kollontai secured extensive changes in marriage laws, maternity and child care provision, and abortion on demand was important.

There was still though a lack of any theory in the marxist or socialist movement which could clarify the relationships between the sexual division of labour and class exploitation or the significance of the separation of sex from procreation and of the social importance of reproduction. In the absence of such a theory, eugenic ideas of controlling reproduction by stopping people who were unfit from breeding and encouraging the cultivation of a superior species took hold. There was talk of race suicide, of birth strikes, of the white middle class – mysteriously always synonymous with superiority – being over-run by the unfit poor. Eugenics had not only conservative imperialist support and a social engineering Fabian wing, it also influenced people on the left who were concerned to find a theory of reproductive control.[26]

Stella Browne was familiar with these debates in Germany and contributed to a book edited by Eden and Cedar Paul, *Population and Birth Control. A Symposium*, in 1917 which included contributions from German socialists. Eden Paul was an ILP member who supported eugenics. He was also interested in early works of sex psychology, reading German and Austrian theorists as well as Ellis. He was concerned both about homosexuality and about the denial of female sexuality. He was a member of the British Society for the Study of Sex Psychology and the Malthusian League.

Cedar Paul was associated with Sylvia Pankhurst's Workers' Suffrage Federation in the First World War. Stella Browne put Cedar Paul in touch with Margaret Sanger in 1917[28] and was later to work with Eden and Cedar Paul in trying to raise sexual questions in the Communist Party.

The combination of sexual radicalism and eugenics was not uncommon. Eugenics appeared to provide a rational system of ordering human procreation. The technical problems of selective breeding were ignored. The relatively rare physical disabilities which were hereditary were confused with acquired characteristics. The political implications of eugenics in terms of race and class power which emerged with the growth of fascism in the 1930s were still not clear.

Through both Eden Paul and Havelock Ellis, Stella Browne was thus aware of the work of the Eugenics Education Society. She occasionally made references to eugenic considerations to give support to her arguments. But as she assumed communists and feminists were the most fit to breed the new race, her interpretation had an ironic twist given the conservatism of many eugenics supporters. She was, however, critical of the Eugenics Education Society's 'class-bias and sex-bias'. They lamented the breeding of the unfit poor and assumed the governing class was fit. They talked of the selfishness of middle-class women in refusing maternity but did not try to improve the position of unmarried mothers or illegitimate children.[29]

The debate between Stella Browne and Kathlyn Oliver in *The Freewoman* was indicative not only of their personal differences on the question of female sexuality but also of quite opposing approaches to feminism. Whereas the main current of late nineteenth century feminism had been to demand access into the world controlled by men by demanding equal rights at work, in education, and the vote, from the early twentieth century women began to concentrate more on biological and domestic oppression.

This tendency within the feminist movement gained momentum after the First World War in Britain. The 'new feminists' insisted that real equality meant recognising the specific predicament of women. They were also aware that feminism implied a challenge to male-dominated culture. The political implications of the new feminism were complex. They made demands for better maternity provision, protection at work, family allowances and sometimes for birth control and abortion. Theoretically they were beginning to consider the significance of women's domestic labour, the consequences of birth control and procreation, the importance of child psychology and children's education. Jane Lewis, commenting on the new feminists working within the National Union of Societies for Equal Citizenship (NUSEC) in the 1920s, describes their political ambiguity:

New feminist theory was potentially radical, recognizing as it did women's necessarily inferior position in a man-made society. However it attempted no analysis of the specific causes of woman's subordinate role in society. New feminists were aware of the special problems facing women who either worked for no pay in the home or performed two jobs, one paid and one unpaid, but they did not realize that work in the family was inseparable from the conditions of exploitation and alienation of commodity producers outside the home. The failure to realize that any real improvement in women's position would necessitate massive changes in the whole structure of society hampered the new feminist programme of action.[30]

Most new feminists looked at particular aspects of women's biological predicament and thought in terms of particular reforms. Like the gradualist socialists who came to support their demands, they tended to regard the state as a neutral force, both in sex and class terms. Thus many of their demands were slowly conceded while being modified with the growth of welfare. Because they had no theoretical means of understanding both what was specific about women's reproductive role in the family, in child-bearing and caring for the husband and children, and the interrelationship of this to the cash-nexus, they tended to present motherhood and domestic labour as an ahistorical condition of essential womanhood.[31] Thus, in trying to give value to what women did by abstracting it from male-dominated capitalism where the measure of value expressed the power of the commodity system, the new feminism fell into the conservatism of asserting a natural and distinct sphere or role. The implications of this were not clear initially. They emerged only when the feminist impulse began to wane from the late 1920s.

Again, Stella Browne was unusual in being influenced by aspects of new feminism without accepting ameliorative welfare, the neutrality of the state or arguing for a separate female sphere. She emerges in the early 1920s, combining a variety of intellectual and political influences; sexual radicalism, free thought, revolutionary syndicalism, marxism, birth control, eugenic ideas of controlling fertility and the new emphasis on women's biological situation within the feminist movement. She was remarkable in her range but not completely alone, for other women and men in the 1920s were on the same tracks. Socialist feminism was a minority tradition within the left. It was nonetheless there.

Birth Control, Abortion and the Left
Between the Wars

This did not mean socialist feminists were always welcomed by the left. Birth control was to become a polarising issue in which they found themselves in conflict with the left as much as the right. Division on the question did not always follow the general differences between left and right.

The working-class movement has a long memory and the old suspicion of Malthusian theories of population control as an alternative to social reform died hard. On the other hand there had been radical advocates of contraception; Robert Dale Owen, Richard Carlile and Charles Knowlton were still remembered in the early twentieth-century socialist movement. There was a long radical tradition of fighting for information about contraception as part of the right to knowledge. Annie Besant and Charles Bradlaugh had faced prosecution for printing Knowlton's *Fruits of Philosophy* in 1877. It is not clear how much connection there was between working-class organisations and birth control agitation after their trial. Historians tend to study movements as institutionally distinct even though the local reality is invariably more confused and interconnected. Heresies are after all likely to resist containment and free enquirers to wander indiscriminately into forbidden places. There are several hints of interest among working-class socialists and radicals in contraception. Investigation might reveal more. For example, though Robert Blatchford, the editor of the popular socialist paper *The Clarion*, was afraid that support for sexual liberation would put people off socialism, a reference to Standring's *Malthusian Handbook* by Julia Dawson in the paper in 1895 produced an extraordinary response. Within six weeks 4,000 copies had been bought through *The Clarion*. Also co-operative libraries sometimes stocked *The Malthusian* in the 1890s. Even before the First World War workers' groups held meetings on birth control. In 1912, Dr Alice Vickery spoke to co-operative women in Tottenham. In 1914, Teresa Billington-Greig, one of the founders of the Women's Freedom League, talked to the Glasgow Clarion Scouts on 'Commonsense on the Population Question'.[32]

So when Rose Witcop and Margaret Sanger nervously held a meeting off the City Road in London in 1920 on 'Birth Control for the Workers',[33] when Stella Browne and Cedar Paul argued in the Communist Party, when a campaign began to get the Labour government to allow welfare nurses in maternity centres to give information about birth control, and Dora Russell with other socialists started the Workers' Birth Control Group, they were within a continuing tradition.

But there was also persistent suspicion among socialists. Margaret Sanger encountered Glasgow socialist men in 1920, 'ready to fight the ancient battle of Marx against Malthus'.[34] Anti-Malthusianism was based on the conviction that birth control was being presented as an alternative to other social changes. There was a real basis for this suspicion. Many members of the Malthusian League were anti-socialist. Drysdale, for example, was opposed to militant labour at the end of the First World War and anti-immigrant. He wanted strikes to be made illegal.[35] Harold Cox, Carpenter's old friend, was against rent control and 'mothers' pensions' – a scheme for extensive family allowances which was being suggested and which would make the mother economically independent. Cox thought they would encourage 'the production of those types who lean upon the State'. He meant, of course, the poor. He saw contraception as a means of reducing the numbers of poor people:

The real danger is that the higher racial or national types may be swamped by the lower types, and the only way of avoiding that danger is by popularising throughout the world the knowledge of how to prevent conception.[36]

People like Cox thus supported birth control campaigns in working-class areas for eugenic reasons. Marie Stopes argued for birth control on the grounds that overcrowding in towns meant 'we have been breeding revolutionaries'.[37] Not surprisingly, this created hostility to contraception among socialists. They saw only the politics of its supporters, not the implications of the issue itself. But these eugenic ideas were not peculiar to birth controllers. Similar arguments the other way around were used in support of family allowances. Eleanor Rathbone wrote to *The Times* during the strike for equal pay of bus conductresses in 1918, urging money for mothers with children from the state:

It would put an end to the increasing practice among all the more thrifty and far-sighted parents deliberately limiting the number of children while slum-dwellers and the mentally unfit continue to breed like rabbits, so that the national stock is recruited in increasing proportions from its least fit elements.[38]

The theoretical opposition to Malthusianism and suspicion of the politics of some supporters of contraception combined with the conviction that workers would become revolutionary through increasing poverty and that preoccupation with 'palliatives' only put off the revolution. This went with a variation on the joke about the Catholic Church opposing birth control in order to keep up members. More babies meant more socialists. Stella Browne was pleased to note when she toured South Wales in 1923 that this argument was becoming less common. In Taff Vale, 'One and one only – voiced the old idea of the necessity of big battalions for the Class War, irrespective of both cost and quality.'[39]

But only the year before she had been involved in a controversy in the paper *The Communist* in which opposition to Malthusianism combined with the argument that birth control was a capitalist quack remedy for unemployment which arose because 'the unemployed today are beginning dimly to be class-conscious'.[40]

The author, writing under the pseudonym of 'Clete', criticised an article by Harold Cox in which he had said no man had the right to become a father who could not maintain the child, 'Clete' argued that 'no decently organised society has the right to deny parenthood to a healthy father'.[41]

Stella Browne then criticised 'Clete' for an 'exclusively masculine point of view'. Comrade 'Clete' had failed to indicate that 'women and mothers were concerned in the matter as well as men and fathers'.[42]

Another correspondent, S. Francis, came to 'Clete's' defence. 'Clete' was not attacking birth control for the individual but gave 'a timely reminder that we should be Marxians first and Malthusians afterwards'.[43] Francis shifts the argument away from Malthusianism to the generally politically-improving character of self-denial:

I do think if women were a little more willing to take their share in the fight against present working class conditions and a little less ready to talk about the evils of child-bearing and the domination of man, we should be nearer to that true equality of the sexes only to be attained when we have established true economic freedom.

On the subject of sex equality, the majority of my women comrades are as unsound as their capitalist-minded sisters. It is time that some of our sex-obsessed comrades realised that woman's so-called 'slavery' to man is solely owing to her economic dependence on him and can only end when the capitalist regime ends.[44]

Francis believed there to be 'other things in life besides the sex act', and was of the opinion,

that if our comrades in general were to spend less of their energy on that, and more on the teaching of Marxian ethics, the CPGB would be a more efficient section of the Third International.[45]

This rare glimpse into the interior of the early Communist Party indicates both the force of feminist feeling in the left after the First World War and the terms in which it was dismissed. The theoretical arguments used to counter feminism denied any autonomy to sexual oppression which was to end automatically with the capitalist mode of production. The determination to reduce sexual questions to economics meant that birth control was seen as an individual matter. Personal life was unimportant. It had to be subordinated to building the party and the party had to present a good front to the Comintern.

Our knowledge of the international policy of the early Communists on the question of women and sexuality remains very sketchy. It is particularly difficult to penetrate the official statement to assess the political debates or conflicts behind decisions. Sexual dissidence had been obscured over the years of interpretation and reinterpretation of the Soviet experience. Both opponents and supporters of leninism and stalinism have tended to bypass these issues as personal rather than political matters. There is also a general problem of working out the relationship between international decree and local practice at different periods of party history. As yet we can only trace the outline of events and surmise attitudes towards sexuality.

In 1921 the congress of the Comintern had decided that there were no 'female' *questions* as all women's issues affected the social position of men. But there were specific female *demands* and there should be special work among women.[46] In October 1922 the CPGB decided they could 'have very little use' for the purely feminist organisations. Their members should work with women in trade unions, the Labour Party and Co-op Guilds. They should try to contact housewives by canvassing, in welfare centres, and through street meetings. 'Prejudice' was acknowledged within the party which would have to be fought 'relentlessly':

Many comrades discourage their wives, sisters and women friends from attending Party meetings, or from taking any part whatever in our work. This attitude must be overcome. Comrades who are adopting it are sabotaging the work of the Party and robbing both Party life and their own family life of half its possibilities.[47]

Again the building of the party becomes an end in itself. The men's behaviour was seen as 'prejudice' not as a response rooted within social relations between the sexes. There is no reference to birth control or to sexual oppression in the report.

Stella Browne had advocated both birth control and abortion at the Fifth International Neo-Malthusian and Birth Control Conference held in London that summer. She spoke 'as a Feminist and a Communist' and had described enthusiastically Kollontai's work in the Soviet Union and the agitation in Germany and Austria led by left-wing feminists and by socialists for birth control: 'for the Continental revolutionary, unlike many of his British brethren, has realised that Birth Control is not a capitalist red herring'.[48]

The conference produced a good deal of comment in the British left press. *Plebs*, the *Daily Herald* and *The Labour Leader* discussed birth control as well as *The Communist*. *The Labour Leader* distinguished birth control, which it supported, from Malthusian doctrine, which it did not.[49] In November 1922 *The New Generation* announced that to show how politically impartial it was, Stella Browne was to be a regular contributor 'to present the Communist case for birth control'. Her point of view was of 'added interest and importance when it is realised that a large number of socialist and working class women think on the same lines'.[50]

Stella Browne based her case on the immediate needs of working-class women, on the communist commitment to sex equality, impossible if women could not choose maternity. She said Cedar Paul understood that economic factors had to be related to 'physical influences'. 'No economic changes would give equality or self-determination to any woman unable to choose or refuse motherhood of her own free will.'

She produced her version of eugenics — lack of militancy among all races was due to ante-natal circumstances and the conditions of conception. She wanted selective birth control to 'produce and build up a race fitted to carry out Communist and Feminist ideals'. The selection though was selection by the individual, not imposed by the state.[51]

Stella Browne was bewildered by the gap between communists' theory and practice:

my most effective and able comrades under the Red Flag practise birth control as intelligently and consistently as any of the politically orthodox. I wish however that the revolutionary women would more boldly and explicitly incorporate birth control not only in their individual tactics but in their philosophy, not for an instant as an alternative solution to the mess the world has got into, but as the accompaniment and aid to our view of life.[52]

Stella Browne left the Communist Party in 1923 because of her different approach to the implications of birth control and abortion.[53] It is still not clear how Communist Party members saw sexual questions in the 1920s or what became of women who were drawn to communism after the First World War 'through awakened sex solidarity and sex ideals'.[54] A correspondent to *The New Generation* in February 1924 claimed to have spoken to a woman communist

who had spoken on birth control at several meetings. 'Oh yes, I have to drop the subject', she said. 'You see the Party haven't discussed the subject so there is no policy declared by the majority. Yes, it is a great pity, the women were very interested. But I must be loyal to the Party.'[55]

Between 1922 and 1924 the British Communist Party was being reshaped in accordance with Comintern instructions. The organisation was centralised, stricter discipline imposed upon members' politics and a stronger emphasis placed on industrial agitation. This involved changes within the power structure. Some of the old guard, prominent in the groups from which the Communist Party had been formed, were eased out. Reorganisation also struck at some of the intellectuals associated with the paper *The Communist* which was seen as too remote from industrial agitation. Educational groups, the Plebs League and the Labour College movement were also affected as both theoretical and practical work were brought under the direct control of the Central Committee of the party.[56]

It is possible that because there was no party line on birth control and abortion, Stella Browne's insistence that she was presenting the communist case produced conflict. Theoretically the denial of the specific nature of sexual oppression meant that birth control and abortion were seen as either unimportant or at best as humane reforms which could alleviate the suffering of working-class women and enable women to be more effective party workers. These appear to have been the grounds on which the Communist Party came round to supporting birth control by the mid 1920s.

But reorganisation was undoubtedly an uneven process. Contradictory stories probably came through about sexual politics in the Soviet Union. It is likely that in some local branches there was a more complex understanding of sexual questions than is reflected in the official statements. There was certainly in some areas a wide context of working-class revolutionary debate struggling with problems of consciousness, subjective and cultural change, psychology and problems of everyday life which could be sympathetic to ideas of sexual liberation. There was also considerable suspicion of leaders, centralisation and a fierce sense of autonomy as a legacy of syndicalism. Communists cannot have been apart from this ferment. It was after all part of their own immediate political tradition and yielded awkwardly to 'Bolshevisation'. Occasionally dissidence surfaces.

In the autumn of 1923, for example, Stella Browne went off to lecture in the Rhondda, South Wales, invited by the Mardy, Ferndale and Tylerstone propaganda committee of the CP and with Eden and Cedar Paul's personal recommendation. In Taff Vale she encountered workers who quoted 'Nietzsche and Havelock Ellis as well as Karl Marx'. She reported that in her talks there she 'aimed at synthesising the theory and practice of birth control with Socialist principles, quite independently of the Malthusian axiom about the ratios of food and population increase'.[51] She stressed the commitment of the Soviet government and used the old free thinking radical demand of knowledge for the workers. She related birth control to housing, lack of education and unemployment. Birth control was the key to a new sexual ethics in which voluntary and conscious parenthood, especially motherhood, was fundamental. It was important for 'the race' and for 'honest and dignified relationships between men and women'. She had opposition from her one defender of 'big battalions for the Class War' and from someone who accepted birth control but thought 'the sex function or sex impulse'[58] should not be stressed. She gave four meetings to between 250 and 300 people. Two meetings were for women only when she talked about methods: 'every foot of floor space was packed and women, mostly with babies clasped in their arms, stood five deep in rows behind the chairs'.[59]

Stella Browne remembered their interest, passionate gratitude and hopefulness. In a later tour in Monmouthshire, supported by local Labour parties this time, it was the same story. She stood on a precarious chair while the women held their babies, some standing throughout the two hours of the meeting:

How often in this tour have elderly women not said, 'You've come too late to help me, Comrade, but give me some papers for my girls. I don't want them to have the life I've had.'[60]

Throughout the agitation for birth control and abortion in the labour movement there was a persistent pressure from women for information. This does not imply that all these women were committed to sexual radical ideas. But the harsh experiences working-class women had to face in pregnancy meant that on birth control and abortion their organisations – the Women's Co-op Guild and the women's section of the Labour Party – were consistently to the left of the male-dominated Labour Party. In 1915 the Women's Co-operative Guild had published *Maternity: Letters from Working*

Women expressing a reluctance to have large families. One woman describes using a 'preventive' and refers to the misery caused by abortifacients. There was also resistance to the husband's assumption of sexual rights over his wife's body.[61]

The attitudes expressed in *Maternity* were reaffirmed when a campaign began in the Labour Party to allow the centres which had been set up under the 1918 Maternity and Child Welfare Act to give advice about birth control as well as about pregnancy. Dora Russell who became involved in this campaign along with Stella Browne and other women in the Labour Party said they 'found that there was so much ignorance about the question and so much feeling among women was being stifled'.

When the issue was raised at the Labour Women's Conference in 1924 people were astonished by,

the intense hostility shown by women to bearing children. It was regarded as the great joy of every mother and the noble work of womanhood and there they were, all getting up and saying they couldn't stand it, they weren't going to have it and they must have it limited.[62]

The actual circumstances of working-class women's sexual and maternal lives belied the myth of motherhood. Dora Russell suggests that their general social situation and the lack of adequate birth control meant that sexual pleasure was very rare. Women would resort to the only forms of control available, evasion and rejection, in order to protect themselves from the terror of an unwanted pregnancy. Although it is very difficult to know what was felt about such a personal experience, the public support for contraception and later for abortion showed that many working-class women were certainly dissatisfied with a life of continuing child-bearing. It is not clear the extent to which this was an immediate practical response to hardship and poverty or whether young working-class women were beginning to feel that they should have the right to control their own fertility.

There were certainly some women in the Labour Party who saw birth control as a political feminist question and not only as an answer to a practical need. Dora Russell writes that she and other young women in the labour movement felt that the issues of sex and maternity could not be evaded:

> there could be no true freedom for women without the emancipation of *mothers* . . . we embarked on a political birth control campaign about which very little is known today. We held – at that date a strange opinion – that a woman had the right to decide how many children she would have, and therefore should receive – as of right – contraceptive advice as an integral part of the service of Maternity and Child Health.[63]

The Workers' Birth Control Group was formed by Dora Russell and other socialists in 1924. It propagandised within the 'Labour, Socialist and Co-operative movement', repudiating 'any suggestion that the working classes are less fit to breed children than other classes, but bases its appeal solely on the grounds that all women, rich or poor, have an equal right to this knowledge'.[64] It was explicitly opposed to the eugenicism current within the birth control movement.

Although influenced by the private clinics started by Marie Stopes and others, the Workers' Birth Control Group wanted birth control to be provided by the state rather than by voluntary effort. Dora Russell stresses also that they saw birth control, the right to refuse motherhood, as part of the general improvement in the conditions in which women could be mothers. She says, 'despite sentiment about maternal joys', mothers were in reality 'the most despised and neglected section of society'.[65] The working-class women in the Labour Party at their conferences, in voting for birth control, showed they knew this all too well.

A similar pattern of agitation was to be repeated in the

1930s to legalise abortion. Stella Browne was in a minority, advocating abortion from 1915. She was influenced by Havelock Ellis but saw abortion as part of a woman's control over her own sexuality not as a means of preventing the 'unfit' from reproducing. She spoke for birth control and abortion in the 1920s but accepted the tactics of concentrating on birth control for the time being. She was content with opposing attempts to make abortion punishable by even harsher penalties like a clause in the Children and Young Persons Protection Bill in 1924 which was supported by the feminist Six Point Group.

During the 1920s there was a tactical difference between birth controllers who thought that abortion would divert attention from the fight for contraception advice in welfare centres and the supporters of abortion who included Alice Jenkins and Janet Chance as well as Browne. The disagreement was not only a matter of political opinion but of personal style. Dora Russell, who thought then that they should concentrate on contraception first, writes in *The Tamarisk Tree*:

Janet Chance had a reassuring respectable air, but Stella Browne was a holy terror. She made no bones about raising the abortion issue at meetings, and, wisps of hair floating down from her untidy coiffure would resist all efforts of a Chairman to put her down. Though I feared harm to our cause, I did glory in her intransigence.[66]

Stella Browne was strengthened in her intransigence by her knowledge of discussion and agitation in the socialist movement in Austria and Germany and by the remarkable changes made in the Soviet Union in the period immediately after the revolution which continued during the 1920s.

Although the international situation had changed by the mid-1930s the campaign for birth control in Britain had made it more possible to raise the abortion issue. In January

1936 Browne formed the tiny Abortion Law Reform Association with Janet Chance, Alice Jenkins, Freda Laski and Dora Russell among the executive.[67] Two years before the Women's Co-operative Guild had passed overwhelmingly a resolution to legalise abortion and an amnesty for women in prison for performing abortions.[68] Working-class women's organisations thus continued to be more radical on sexual questions than the male-dominated Labour Party.

Writing about the 1925 Labour Party conference's discussion of birth control, where the Labour women's resolution had been defeated with 1,850,000 votes against and 1,530,000 for, Dorothy Jewson said,

Even at the Conference, if there had been as good a representation of mothers as there was of fathers, there is no doubt what the verdict would have been, for there is no subject on which women feel with such passionate earnestness at the present time.[69]

She thought the Labour Party's dismissal of this resolution was part of a wider disregard for the women. 'It is no new thing for the women of the Labour Party to find questions of particular interest to themselves placed at the end of a long agenda'.[70]

Dora Russell in the 1920s felt the Labour Party was 'dominated by masculine perspective' and that this contributed to women's political apathy.[71] George Lansbury's daughter, Dorothy Thurtle, another campaigner for birth control and later for abortions, said that the Executive Committee of the Labour Party,

only have any use for women so long as they have no opinions of their own but are willing to do the donkey work of the Party. Some of us do not agree that our function as Labour women is merely to help a few Labour men make careers and sit on the Government Front Bench, and I ask those women in the Party who think that our men must *on all questions* make a stand on principle and not expediency to let their prospective candidates and sitting Members know their opinion.[72]

Male resistance against women's specific oppression thus was one factor. Stella Browne expressed exasperation because over and over again she had to 'refute the cheerful assertion of some masculine wage-earners, that to bear and rear children was *all* women had to do'.[73]

Another expediency which affected the Labour leadership was the importance of the working-class Catholic vote and the organisation of Catholics both within and outside the Labour Party. The Catholic Women's League opposed the campaign for birth control advice at maternity welfare centres. In 1926 the League of National Life was formed to combat the theory and practice of birth control which they regarded as a national peril. Its members were nearly all Catholics or Anglo-Catholics.[74]

It was more convenient for the Labour leadership to play ostrich and not to combat either male sexism or the Catholic Church. Male domination and political opportunism were not of course the grounds on which they openly blocked the pro-birth control lobby. The old theoretical arguments were still around. Birth control as a ruling class '"blind" used to distract the workers'[75] or Blatchford's old preoccupation with economics first, sex later, continued to have some currency in the 1920s.[76] Nor had Malthus' ghost been laid.

Ramsay MacDonald was quite prepared to play on anti-Malthusianism in blocking the pressure for birth control. His other tactic was to dismiss the political aspect of voluntary motherhood and reduce birth control to a private, health issue.[77] The official attitude was put by the chair at the 1925 conference:

the subject of Birth Control is in its nature not one which should be made a political Party issue, but should remain a matter upon which members of the Party should be free to hold and promote their individual convictions.[78]

Dora Russell states that this 'attitude of the Labour Party that sex questions had no place in politics'[79] was one of the obstacles faced by Labour women who tried to raise birth control as a political demand. Socialist feminists thus met opposition both from reformist socialists and from marxists.

The Victorian notion of a separate sphere for women still lingered in the Labour Party in the 1920s. The Labour leadership's view that birth control was a private matter echoed ironically the Liberal leader Gladstone's refusal to consider women's suffrage as a political question forty years before.

In 1884 he had said votes for women was:

One of those questions which it would be intolerable to mix up with purely political and Party debates. If there be a subject in the whole compass of human life and experience that is sacred, beyond all other subjects, it is the character and position of women.[80]

Feminist pressure made it increasingly difficult for politicians to oppose all reforms in women's position. But MacDonald, who had been as horrified by the militant suffragettes as he was by the syndicalists' emphasis on direct action, was cautious and conservative about relations between the sexes. The description of his own relationship with his wife Margaret MacDonald, which he wrote just after she died in 1912, was consistent with this:

To turn to her in stress and storm was like going into a sheltered haven where waters were at rest and smiling up into the face of heaven weary and worn, buffeted and discouraged . . . I would flee . . . and my lady would heal and soothe me with her cheery faith and steady conviction, and send me forth to smite and be smitten.[81]

Such Ruskinian views had already made him an opponent of the minority strand within feminism which questioned the family. In January 1912 *The Freewoman* attacked 'the pontifical pronouncement of Mr Ramsay MacDonald that socialism must preserve the family as the social unit, meaning of course the patriarchal family as by law established, with its subordination of the wife and children to the father'.[82]

Stella Browne pointed out in 1927 that MacDonald's denial of women's right to birth control as a political question was not consistent with his view of socialism as a movement which was not purely economic but involved change in the quality of life.[83] He was prepared to invoke ideals against marxist opponents but forgot all about them when it came to an issue which threatened men's control over women in the family.

It was not only MacDonald and the labour leadership who were reluctant to see the relationship between the sexes as a political question. There was also opposition from the left Clydeside MPs. Dora Russell says:

The Clydeside MPs accused us of telling the working classes that they couldn't have so many children because they were poor; we replied that it's not a question of economics, or of the best stock, it's simply a woman's question in relation to her husband.[84]

Labour women in the Workers' Birth Control Group believed that working-class women should have more money *and* birth control, not either/or. 'We asserted that even if we lived in Buckingham Palace we would not want a baby every year.'[85]

However, the non-marxist socialism of the Independent Labour Party was never a consistent body of doctrine and remained more open to ideas about immediate changes in personal living than the marxism of the Communist Party in Britain in the early 1920s. The idealist or romantic socialists were more concerned about the quality of existence and the transformation of everyday life. Such an emphasis had radical implications for feminism and sexual politics and the nucleus for the agitation for birth control in welfare clinics came from socialists in and around the ILP. There was a most determined group of women who, besides Stella Browne, included Dora Russell, Dorothy Jewson, Dorothy Thurtle, Alice Hicks, Jennie Baker, Margaret Lloyd, Freda Laski, Joan Allen and Leah L'Estrange Malone. It was still regarded as shocking for unmarried women to demand birth control so Browne and Jewson, who were single, were particularly courageous. Ellen Wilkinson told Dora Russell that she really supported the birth controllers but 'had to be careful as unmarried'[86] – though she did vote in favour of Thurtle's bill in 1926.

Birth control was an embarrassing issue because it did not simply seek an improvement in the position of working-class women as wives and mothers, it carried an implicit challenge to relations between men and women within the working class. Labour women who had been willing to support other reforms for women, for example Katharine Glasier who fought for maternity leave or Ethel Bentham who had supported baby clinics before the First World War, would not support the birth control campaign. There were, however, socialist men who were active. These included ex-suffrage supporters George Lansbury, H.G.Wells, Bertrand Russell and Harold Laski and several MPs, Ernest Thurtle (Shoreditch), F.A.Broad (Edmonton), S.Viant (Willesden West), W.M.Adamson (Cannock Chase) and J.Baker (Bilston).

Support came from the rank and file of the ILP and the

Labour Party, especially from the women's sections, from the Women's Co-op Guilds, from Trades Councils, local TU branches and Unemployed Workers' groups. There are many questions which remain unanswered about the extent of this feeling and without a much fuller local history of the socialist movement in this period it is difficult to assess how the demand was seen politically. There were some areas, Battersea for instance, where the connection was most persistent between birth control agitation and the labour movement. There are hints of a theoretical interest in sex reform from Stella Browne's account of her tour of South Wales. There are possibly some links with the suffrage campaign locally. There must have been other working-class women like Hannah Mitchell, active in the Women's Social and Political Union and later the Women's Freedom League, who went into the Labour Party after the war and wished that birth control advice had been available when they were young.[87]

Jessie Stephen, another socialist feminist who had been in the WSPU in Glasgow and worked for Sylvia Pankhurst's Workers Suffrage Federation, became involved in the Workers' Birth Control Group. She was influenced not only by her feminism but by the experience of her own mother. The birth control campaign was not only a matter of the public politics of meetings, resolutions and delegations, it touched the intimate and private lives of women who were never part of the conscious, active labour movement. Jessie Stephen remembers:

You know my mother used to speak to me being the eldest, you see. She'd say 'I don't know. I wish I didn't have all these babies'. I said 'Why don't you do something about it'. She says, 'Oh no he says it's not natural'. A socialist, mind you and he hadn't learned enough about that. It so happened that a few months later, I came across a book which gave you all the information and I handed it to my mother. I said 'Now mother here's your chance, read this.' She was forty-two at the time and she didn't have the menopause till she was fifty-four. She had no more children though. That's what you call teaching grandma to suck eggs.[88]

However, the initiative for the birth control campaign did not come from the post-war feminist organisation, the National Union of Societies for Equal Citizenship, though old suffragettes Mrs Pethick Lawrence and Mrs Chapman gave some support. This was partly because of the continuing feminist suspicion of sexual demands and the concern to make women equal to men in society as it was. There was, however, pressure within NUSEC for changes in the position of mothers. The 'new feminists', Eleanor Rathbone, Maude Royden and Mary Stocks, advocated family allowances as a means of giving the woman enough to support herself and her children. The general ideas of the new feminists on the need to make demands which would change women's biological predicament and their criticisms of equalitarian feminists who concentrated on bringing women into a men's world were part of the cultural and political assumptions of socialist feminists like Browne and Russell. But there were some crucial differences. Apart from Mary Stocks, the new feminists in NUSEC did not make any connection at first between birth control and family allowances as two aspects of women's control over reproduction. In 1925 they added birth control to their demands but it remained a nominal issue until 1927. Also Rathbone saw family allowances as a means of strengthening the family and it was in this context that they were introduced by Beveridge after the Second World War.[89]

Birth control as a single issue campaign was to advance shorn of its connections with the left. Within the New Generation League and Marie Stopes' Society for Constructive Birth Control and Racial Progress there had always been people who saw birth control as a means of stabilising capitalist society. By the late 1920s liberal women Ursula Williams and Margery Spring-Rice had become advocates of birth control in welfare centres. In 1930 a National Birth Control Association was formed and this became the Family Planning Association in 1939.

The idea of birth control as a means of planning families in a planned society was very different from Stella Browne's view of birth control as one aspect of women's sexual self-determination. In the 1930s she shifted her own efforts towards the legalisation of abortion. In the tradition established by birth controllers in the 1920s, the Abortion Law Reform Association turned in 1936 to the Women's Co-operative Guild and the feminist National Council for Equal Citizenship for support.

The emergence of a more moderate political context for the demand for birth control was part of wider changes within capitalist society, in working-class patterns of work and family life. The greater significance of the sphere of reproduction, the direct intervention of the state in the form of welfare provision are reflected in a shift in attitudes towards conception, child-rearing and the family. The early connection between birth control and women's control over their own sexuality was obscured. The eugenic assumptions about preventing the 'unfit' from having large families, and the liberal enthusiasm for small families as effective units for reproduction within capitalism prevailed, providing a new ideology of family planning.[90]

Section 3
**The Campaign for Birth Control
in the Labour Movement**

Concern for the conditions of motherhood, of which birth control was one aspect, had a confused political background in the early twentieth century, in which pressure from some feminists and labour women for free motherhood combined with an eugenic lobby which urged that reproduction was the affair of the state.[91] The 1918 Maternity and Child Welfare Act provided for advice and help for pregnant women. But although the infant mortality rate declined, the maternal mortality rate did not. Indeed it actually became more dangerous to give birth between 1922 and 1933. In the 1920s around 39,000 women died in childbirth in England and Wales.[92] The young Labour women campaigning for birth control produced the slogan 'It is four times as dangerous to bear a child as to work in a coal mine.' In fact they understated their own case.[93] The maternal mortality rate did not fall until the 1940s.

In the same period there was a marked decline in family size. Though most evident among the middle class – much to the eugenicists' distress – it also affected the working class. Around the end of the nineteenth century fewer than 20 per cent of all families had less than three children. By the 1930s only 19 per cent of all families had more than three. While economic pressure and the increased availability of contraception contributed to these smaller families, the decline indicated deeper social changes in the working class, reflected in the women's determination not to reproduce their mothers' lives of ceaseless pregnancy, in overcrowded conditions. Women between the two world wars wanted smaller families and the decline in the birth rate was the statistical expression of their new attitude to conception and child-rearing.[94]

The actual methods of birth control which people used and how they heard of them remains remarkably mysterious even for this recent period. Propagandists for birth control and abortion probably tended to over-stress ignorance and enquiry would reveal a hidden folk knowledge of preventive measures. Despite the birth controllers' efforts to diffuse information about the Mensinga diaphragm most women undoubtedly used forms of contraception which only *lessened* the likelihood of pregnancy.[95] Many women relied on home-made devices. The vaginal sponge was a very old form of contraception which Jessie Stephen describes still being used in the 1920s:

There was a fine sponge with a silk thread attached to it, soaked in quinine and linseed oil, but preferably olive oil because it didn't smell so. They had to insert this, and immediately after intercourse, they pulled this down because they'd impregnated the womb with this stuff and that prevented conception.[96]

Norman E.Hines, reporting on the work of the birth control clinics in 1928, lists several forms of contraception which were being used before women came to the clinics – pessaries, douching or sponges. But in using these methods it could not be assumed that intercourse would not lead to pregnancy. The other popular methods, coitus interruptus and sheaths, meant relying on the man.[97] In this situation abortion and infanticide were the last resort for women desperate to control their fertility.

Illegal abortion is notoriously difficult to quantify for only those that fail become statistics. It is possible that abortion — sometimes euphemistically described as miscarriage — was a more common feature of working-class women's lives than is commonly imagined. Against the stereotype of the sinister quack luring women to have unwanted abortions for large sums of money, the picture which emerges from the Interdepartmental Committee on Abortion in 1938 is of women who aborted themselves or relied on someone known and trusted within the community. Drugs were obtained from herbalists, chemists or stalls in market places. Women heard of them by word of mouth or advertisements or booklets — one of which was called *The Shadow of the Stork*. Women passed enema syringes round the village or round a factory.[98] This hidden history of control over reproduction could well have been transmitted from generation to generation. It did represent a means of women deciding how many children they could care for, and the campaigners for legal abortion have perhaps blackened the picture by stressing the failures. For every abortion that failed, resulting in death or serious illness, there must have been many which went unrecorded because they were successful.

If the dangers of illegal abortion were exaggerated this did not mean they were not real. Abortion under these conditions was still risky and dangerous. The women who took large doses of Beechams Pills, castor oil, a dessert spoonful of mustard in a pint of stout, nutmeg or saltpetre or washing powder in gin or penny-royal only aborted by making themselves very ill. The abortifacients did not have a specific effect on the uterus, but acted as 'general poisons causing convulsions or vomiting which produces abortion as a side effect'.[99] This, along with damage caused by the insertion of objects like knitting needles, hair pins, crochet hooks, a skewer used to fix bobbins in a mill, must have contributed to long-term ill-health and could have affected subsequent pregnancies. Some were fatal. Between 1926 and 1935 around 500 women died every year from abortion. Even despite the danger, in the absence of reliable contraception and safe legal abortion, women continued to use the old methods of abortion in order not to have large families. There was concern between the wars that abortion, along with maternal mortality, was increasing and that the two were not unconnected.[100] This was an important impetus for pressure both for birth control and later for legal abortion.

The Malthusian League had been a propagandist force for birth control in working-class areas before and immediately after the First World War. The League favoured the Mensinga pessary or dutch cap.[101] In the autumn of 1920 Anna Martin began to teach women in Rotherhithe about birth control methods, continuing Dr Alice Vickery's earlier work. She found many of the women had already practised birth control on their own account. The problem was not just one of information but of availability of reliable contraception.[102]

In 1921 Marie Stopes opened her clinic in Holloway, North London, where she fitted a high-domed cervical cap.[103] A few months later Norman Haire, a gynaecologist, opened the East Street Centre for Pre-Maternity, Maternity and Child Welfare in Walworth.[104] A new era of practical agitation had begun. *The New Generation* carried reports of the response of the women to the clinic in South London. Stella Browne wrote of her hope that women in 'Co-op Guilds' and 'Labour Groups' would become involved in agitation for birth control and it was to these groups that she turned for support.[105] Besides Kollontai's work in the Soviet Union, Margaret Sanger was an important inspiration. Browne knew of Sanger's links with the American socialist movement, and her own knowledge of the international connection between sex reform and socialism was strengthened by Sanger's accounts of her reception by workers in Germany and Austria.[106] It was a reciprocated relationship. Kollontai read *The New Generation* and arranged to visit the Walworth clinic in 1925 and Sanger published Stella Browne in her birth control journal.[107] There was also a personal friendship with a woman who had helped Browne to understand the struggle of working-class women against the 'double burden of economic conditions and a bondage to reproduction'.

She was the mother of thirteen children, two of these died in early youth and two were born dead – one prematurely. She had also two miscarriages. Of the nine survivors, she made a useful self-respecting group of men and women, with a good share of happiness and quick intelligence, though none were very robust. Between forty and fifty she was infected with syphilis by her second husband whom she mainly supported. She lost the sight of one eye and suffered terribly from ulcers, for of course prompt and adequate treatment was out of the question in her case.[108]

She acted nonetheless as a 'tower of mental and psychic strength and a source of help and happiness to many distressed and unhappy people'. Stella Browne realised that, despite these gifts, her friend would be among those seen by eugenicists as 'unfit' to have children. Browne felt that this woman would have been celebrated if she had had the circumstances and encouragement 'lavished on any blockhead born into the classes which arrogate to themselves the name "fit"'.[109]

Very little is known of Stella Browne's personal life and so this is a rare glimpse of an early friendship which had a deep and lasting influence on her politics. She felt a personal commitment to her friend and through her to 'the woman worker who loves and helps and thinks'.[110] The women the League were to help were the 'sisters' of her own friend.

Throughout the 1920s and 1930s the numbers of voluntary birth control clinics increased. The Walworth group encouraged the formation of local groups out of which clinics could develop. They opened in several parts of London, followed by Wolverhampton in 1925; Manchester and Salford, East London, Glasgow, Oxford and Aberdeen in 1926; Birmingham in 1927; Rotherham in 1928; Newcastle on Tyne in 1929; Exeter, Nottingham and Pontypridd in 1930 and Bristol and Ashington in Northumberland in 1931.

The impulse behind the clinics varied. There were Malthusian and eugenic reasons for birth control for workers. Sometimes they were formed by rich women who gave money on a charity basis. Feminists and socialists were involved too – in Glasgow the clinic was formed by Labour and Co-operative women, and received funds from local trade union branches. A member of the Workers' Birth Control Group, Alice Hicks, made the appointments. Particular economic distress and industrial conflict had an effect. Birth controllers in the Cannock Chase colliery district near Wolverhampton became involved after the General Strike in informing miners' wives about contraceptives during the lock-out. The Rotherham, Newcastle and Pontypridd clinics were also in mining areas.[111]

The study carried out by Norman Hines in the summer of 1927 showed that most women who attended clinics were working class. Women tended to come in their early thirties, when they had already had around three children. They were from both the skilled and unskilled working class. Many of them had had what were described as 'natural' abortions.[112] But the clinics could only advise a minority, if an important minority. Because they were dependent on voluntary aid their existence was precarious. They were vulnerable to accusations. It was implied that the women who started clinics were loose and immoral. The Catholic press said the Manchester and Salford birth controllers were 'the kind of women who visit matinees and sit with cigarettes between their painted lips'.[113] Other attacks were that they were making money or using working-class women as victims in 'experiments'.

The Maternity and Infant Welfare Centres which had been set up under the 1918 Act seemed to form a basis for extending birth control instruction. Towards the end of 1922 a member of the Malthusian League, Miss E.S.Daniels, a health visitor in Edmonton, North London, was suspended by her Medical Officer for giving the address of Marie Stopes' clinic and of the New Generation League. On 19 December 1922 she was dismissed for insubordination at a meeting of the Edmonton Urban Council. A deputation from the Unemployed Women's Committee led by Mrs Porteous came to the meeting. They had organised a petition in support of Nurse Daniels and in favour of provision for birth control. It must have been a stormy encounter with the chairman of the Maternity Committee, Councillor Elms, accusing Miss Daniels of being an agent for selling contraceptives. The verdict against her was passed by 13 votes to 7.

This local decision was supported by Janet Campbell at the Ministry of Health. Maternity and Infant Welfare Centres should deal only with expectant mothers and nursing mothers and infants, not with married or unmarried women thinking of contraception. Only when avoidance of pregancy was desirable on medical grounds should women be referred for contraceptive advice and then to a GP or in exceptional circumstances to a hospital.[114]

Neither Edmonton Urban Council nor the Ministry of Health could realise the opposition this decision was going to create. They had provided a focus for the energies of the birth control campaigners and a means by which birth control could be taken as a directed campaign to local Labour and trade-union groups. In 1922–23 birth control was very much in the news. Marie Stopes was locked in conflict with Catholic opponents who she had sued for libel. Rose Witcop and Guy Aldred had published and distributed Margaret Sanger's *Family Limitation* in 1922. This was seized by the police on an obscenity charge. The grounds for the charge were somewhat bizarre. Dora Russell became involved in the defence of *Family Limitation* and relates:

The pamphlet said, among other things, that women should have pleasure in sexual intercourse, a point which I observed was displeasing to the Bench, who were, perhaps, thinking of their wives and daughters. There was also a diagram showing how, with the finger, to place a Dutch pessary in the vagina. Obscenity, we were advised, lay in the fact that this might not be the woman's own finger. Not having a sufficiently dirty mind, this had not occurred to me or to others.[115]

The case raised the eugenic objections to birth control and the complaint that it was 'against nature'. It became a focus for agitation which united members of the Malthusian League with socialists and feminists. Dora and Bertrand Russell were important in this connection. At a meeting in Essex Hall in March 1923, Bertrand Russell spoke together with Dr Drysdale, Guy Aldred, Nurse Daniels and the old suffragette, Mrs E.Pethick Lawrence. In the trial Aldred conducted his own defence based on the old radical demand of the right to knowledge, telling the court he followed in the footsteps of Carlile and Bradlaugh.[116] They lost their case. Aldred said he wanted to take the case to the High Court but Rose Witcop saw birth control in terms of direct action tactics and dismissed constitutionalism. This had been Margaret Sanger's initial approach in America and tallied with Witcop's anarchism. She was increasingly committed to birth control as her main form of political action.[117] *Family Limitation* was reprinted in 1924 without the offending finger, in defiance of the court case, but it was not seized again.[118] Witcop subsequently opened a clinic in Shepherds Bush.

The free union of Rose Witcop and Guy Aldred was disintegrating. By the early '20s they were emotionally and politically moving apart though a few years later they were married formally to prevent her being deported. Direct action was not to be the form of birth control agitation in Britain. Instead, the campaign developed in 1923 to put pressure on the Labour Party to change the decision against Nurse Daniels and allow the welfare centres to give birth control advice. Stella Browne was deeply involved in this campaign from the start. It revealed both the willingness of local Labour groups to discuss sexual questions and the determination of women in the Labour Party to agitate for birth control against all the attempts of the leadership to block and silence them.

Stella Browne spoke in March 1923 for the Raynham Road Women's Co-op Guild in Upper Edmonton, explaining practical contraceptive methods to around fifty women. The meeting passed a unanimous resolution 'demanding the cessation of birth control prosecution and provision of reliable information at Government Welfare Centres', which they sent to the Home Secretary and the Ministry of Health.[119] It was the beginning of several hundred meetings on the subject. In 1923 Stella Browne spoke at Chelsea Trades Council and Labour Party, East Ham Women's

Co-op Guild, at Limehouse Town Hall for the National Unemployed Workers' Committee, at St Albans Women's Adult School, at meetings of Clapham, North Kensington, Fulham and Chelsea, Poplar, Paddington, Kennington, and Parsons Green branches of the Women's Co-op Guild, to the Central Labour College, at the suggestion of Comrade Howell Morgan, to the Women's Section of the National Union of General Workers in Fulham and the Battersea Branch of the same union.[120] The women in Fulham wanted not only birth control advice but change in the law on abortion to recognise 'women's right to terminate an undesired pregnancy'. Although many of the women were unemployed, they insisted on taking a collection and 6s6d was raised for the Walworth Women's Welfare Centre.[121] Stella Browne met Dorothy Jewson at this meeting and convinced her of the need to support birth control.[122] After her meeting in Battersea on the 'Socialist Case for Birth Control', Stella Browne led a meeting for the Unemployed Workers' Organisation in Battersea. The Battersea Labour Party appointed a special sub-committee to agitate for a birth control centre. They received no help from the Ministry of Health – Stella Browne nicknamed it the Ministry of Disease – so were thinking of forming a private centre.[123]

Besides this work in London, Stella Browne was busy with her tours of Wales in the autumn and winter of 1923. In the Workmen's Institute Temperance Hall Tredegar, she spoke on 'Birth Control in its Relation to Socialism' to an audience of 900:

The audience listened eagerly to my account of the recent history of the movement. They groaned as I told them of the underhand attempts in this country to suppress among the poor, the knowledge freely available to the wealthy, and described the prosecution of the working class Aldreds for publishing a pamphlet whose author had been feted in London five months before. They cheered when I described the rally of the brains and hands of the labour movement to the defence of the right to knowledge. They were equally interested to hear of the struggle abroad, the savage repression in France, the vindication of women's fundamental rights in Russia, the constructive propaganda among German socialists and communists.[124]

She also addressed women's meetings on practical methods in several other towns in South Wales. In 1924 the same pattern of agitation continued. The close links with Battersea continued. Stella Browne did meetings for South Battersea Labour Party, Battersea Branch of the Amalgamated Engineering Union, Battersea Amalgamated Wheelwrights, Smiths and Kindred Trades and Lavender Hill Women's Section of the Labour Party. She spoke in a converted synagogue to Stoke Newington Labour Party surrounded by Walter Crane drawings, to a Women's Section of the Labour Party in Ealing and to a meeting for Chiswick AEU.

Lack of money made it difficult to get out of London, but she did manage a tour of East Anglia early in the year, invited by the Norwich Labour Party and Dr Violet Jewson, and meetings at St Albans and Feltham, Middlesex.[125]

Stella Browne's speaking engagements, which continued throughout the 1920s, give an indication of the interest in the subject among Labour and trade-union groups and particularly among women.

In May 1924 Dora Russell, Jennie Baker and Stella Browne were among a delegation to Wheatley, Labour Minister of Health, who was assisted by Dr Janet Campbell. Stella Browne could not understand how Campbell, 'herself a woman' and aware of the conditions of maternity, could 'sit unmoved through the evidence and continue service under the Ministry after our deputation'.[126] In fact several prominent labour women were opposed to birth control, including Mrs Harrison Bell, Ethel Bentham and Marion Phillips, the Labour Party women's organiser.

Wheatley was also unmoved by Dora Russell who 'spoke from the feminist socialist point of view',[127] by Jennie Baker who spoke of her experience in women's guilds and in the Finchley Women's Section of the Labour Party. Himself a Catholic socialist, he refused to change the order against birth control in welfare centres or to allow doctors to give birth control as part of the National Health Service. His grounds were religious feelings which would object to public funds being used for the centres to provide birth control. He told them it could not be an administrative decision and had to be changed by parliamentary sanction.

Dora Russell 'obviously on fire with indignation at such callous quibbling, rose more than once to heckle him'.[128] Another delegate, 'Alderman Reed', tried to protest but Wheatley 'peremptorily silenced' him 'in a manner' which Stella Browne, always alert to male authoritarianism, observed was 'suggestive of the school master'.[129] It is likely Wheatley saw 'Alderman Reed' as a more familiar opponent than determined socialist feminists like Russell and Browne. Stella Browne commented – prophetically in Wheatley's case – that 'the Clyde Democracy has a way of evaporating'.

In 1923 the Chelsea and Epsom Labour Women's Sections had sent in two resolutions in favour of birth control in welfare centres. By 1924 Chelsea and Epsom had been joined by Forest Gate, North Lambeth, St Pancras North, Greenwich, Battersea North and South, Finchley, Ipswich, Grimsby, Nelson, North Edinburgh. The Labour Women's conference early in the year voted overwhelmingly in favour of birth control, by 1,000 to 8.[130] There was another unsuccessful deputation to Wheatley from the Standing Joint

Committee of Industrial Women's Organisations.[131] Support began to develop in local Labour Parties in 1924. In October *The New Generation* reported that at least eleven party branches had sent in resolutions, more in fact than on any other issue. They were from Hendon, Shoreditch, North Kensington, South Kensington, Chelsea Trades Council, NE Bethnal Green, Southend, East Lewisham, Brighton and Hove and Chester-le-Street.[132] Dora Russell writes in her autobiography, *The Tamarisk Tree*, 'Mr Wheatley had stirred a hornet's nest: all through 1924 we buzzed and stung'.[133] The Workers' Birth Control Group was formed in that year.

The birth controllers made a dramatic intervention. Mr W.Thorne in the chair made what Stella Browne described as a 'singularly unfortunate remark to the effect that "the ladies wish to lecture us on birth control and restraining our animal passions"'.[134] In fact, nine of the delegates from Labour Party branches were men – apart from Stella Browne only the delegate from Chester-le-Street was a woman. Stella Browne protested at the chair's comment and was supported by angry noises throughout the hall. Thorne had to apologise. But the birth control resolution was defeated.[135]

The women's organiser of the Labour Party, Dr Marion Phillips, had tried to stop Dora Russell supporting birth control on the grounds that sex should be kept out of politics and that the issue would split the party. From which Dora Russell concluded that the role of women's organiser was to keep women members in order rather than to fight for women's issues.[136] After the second deputation to Wheatley in 1924 Phillips suggested an enquiry into birth control, which was a way of stalling the question. She was to come round to the demand by the end of 1925 because of sustained pressure from women within the party.

The women were already impatient with official blocking of their campaign. In 1925 the Labour Women's conference re-affirmed their support. This time 15 local Labour Parties backed the demand at the Party conference. This was more than any other resolution except communist affiliation. Indeed the executive saw the birth controllers as another example of communist pressure.[137]

Support by 1925 was less concentrated in London, though with E.Thurtle in Shoreditch and the communist MP Saklatvala in Battersea, there were places continuing to be pro-birth control. W.Thorne in Plaistow had also become a supporter after his chastening experience with Stella Browne. Support from Glasgow, T. Henderson, the Co-op MP for the Tradeston Division, and some MPs in the north-east were important regional extensions.[138]

In the autumn of 1925 the New Generation League distributed thousands of leaflets in factories all over the Midlands and Yorkshire. They reported they got most help from local Labour Parties, the ILP, the Co-op Women's Guilds and Working Men's Clubs, only rarely from Conservative and Liberal groups. But Beatrice McCabe's report on the tour remained determinedly middle class and very different in tone from Stella Browne.[139]

By the following year the debate had reached the House of Commons. In February 1926 Ernest Thurtle moved for leave to bring in a Bill for public money to be made available for knowledge to be given to married women. Ellen Wilkinson voted in favour of Thurtle's motion but other Labour women abstained. There was no support from the Clydeside left-wingers, some were against. Thurtle was defeated. This was followed by a surprising vote of support in the Lords.[140] The Workers' Birth Control Group produced a leaflet showing which MPs had voted for and against Thurtle's bill. With the support of the ILP conference in 1926 it went to the constituencies of Labour men who had opposed the motion. Dora Russell spoke at meetings in Consett and Chopwell in the north-east which were organised by a miner, Steve Lawther. Mrs Lawther was also involved in the birth control campaign. Dora Russell and Alice Hicks then set off to Motherwell, the seat of Thurtle's opponent, Rev. James Barr. Dora Russell was carrying 'a whole bale of pamphlets' on birth control which should not really have been classed as passenger luggage. But the railwaymen grinned and bundled it on at the London terminal saying 'We know you, Mrs Russell.'[141] In Motherwell she stayed with a steelworker John Wilson and his wife in their tiny tenement flat:

John Wilson took the chair at our birth control meetings. I can still see him, his head slightly bowed, shy and apprehensive at approaching this subject which to so many was taboo. As I was always to find, once the ice was broken, women spoke out about their sufferings and needs.[142]

This journey to Scotland was followed up by visits to the Welsh mining areas.

At the Labour Party conference in October 1926 Dora Russell demanded, not a vote on birth control itself, but a commitment to the right of the centres to give advice. Dorothy Jewson seconded on behalf of the ILP pointing out that only 70 out of the 1,000 delegates were women and that the women's conferences had voted for it. The two women stood on chairs to address the conference crowded into the Winter Garden at Blackpool. The executive produced Ramsay MacDonald to oppose them. The discussion ended in clamour and confusion when Dr Esther Rickards complained that birth control was a 'side-issue'. Dora Russell's winding-up was inaudible. When the voting came, the executive was beaten by 36,000 votes.[143]

Predictably the Labour executive simply forgot about conference's decision. Between 1926 and 1927 the Catholics organised energetically and secured decisive block trade-union votes. Despite a moving speech by Mrs Lawther, from Blaydon, Durham, urging the miners to support the women and reminding them of the women's support in the strike, this time the birth control resolution was lost. This defeat was repeated at the Labour Women's conference in 1928.[144]

The militancy and zest of the early campaign had gone. The atmosphere changed from 1927. It was as if the defeat of the General Strike and the miners' lock-out had exerted an influence on the birth control campaign. But the need was still there. Birth controllers turned away from the socialist movement, gaining broader support from NUSEC and the Women's National Liberal Federation who were represented at a large conference in April 1930.

Because of this pressure from outside the Labour Party, the Ministry of Health compromised by producing a memorandum saying centres could give advice to married women on medical grounds, if having another baby would harm the woman's health. The memo was not made public until Marie Stopes printed it gleefully in her *Birth Control News* in September 1930.[145] Stella Browne was quick to see that 'medical grounds' could be widely interpreted. 'What', she asked, 'are strictly medical grounds, taking into consideration the effects of under-feeding and over-crowding, and of mind and nerves on the child-bearing function in women?'[146]

Despite the Ministry's efforts to limit the implications of the memo, thirty-six local authorities had decided to take action under the new instructions by the middle of 1931. Slowly a family planning clinic network emerged. It was an important reform to win but the victory seemed a small one in comparison to the tremendous energy which had gone into the campaign. Also the demand for birth control had shed the political meanings which socialist feminists had attached to it. The freer availability of contraception meant that women's sexual lives were somewhat easier. There was more chance of sexual pleasure without fear of pregnancy. But the attempt to transform the circumstances of reproduction, so that women had control over their biological destiny was far from realisation.

Birth control is only one aspect of this sexual self-determination which involves abortion, maternity provision, nurseries, economic freedom and communal ways of caring for children. As birth control became respectable, it became assimilated within the extension of social planning. It was increasingly seen as population control by the state with Malthusian and eugenic undertones. Women's reproductive control receded as the feminist movement dwindled into a series of parliamentary lobbies. In the changed political context of fascism, depression, war and welfarism, the socialist feminism of the period immediately after the First World War seemed disingenuous.

Our Bodies are Our Own

Stella Browne spoke for a generation of young women inspired by the feminist movement before the First World War, determined that change for women would not end with the vote. The bitter experience of the First World War scarred them. Stella Browne observed during the war the most ruthless exploitation of women's capacity to labour and to give birth, with its accompanying praise of the woman wage-earner, followed by the reversal afterwards when unemployed ex-servicemen returned[147] and it was 'once more economically a crime to be a woman'.[148] During the war the social conditions of the women left behind doing war work or living on separation allowances surfaced in reports, surveys and investigations. There was a vague promise of change which was swiftly forgotten in the midst of unemployment in the 1920s.

Writing in 1917 Stella Browne connected the demand for birth control and abortion to a whole series of changes in women's position, which included co-operative housekeeping schemes, good housing, a national health service, better maternity provision, legal changes in the bastardy law, and laws on separation and divorce, national education with sex instruction.[149] Like Margaret Sanger, Browne's experience of the conditions of working-class women also convinced her of the extent of sexual unhappiness and of the need for birth control.[150]

By raising questions of sexuality Stella Browne and other socialist feminists found themselves at odds with both the feminist and socialist movements. Dora Russell said in *The Right to be Happy* in 1925 that it was not astonishing that older feminists went in for 'Purity and Prohibition' and could not 'see what sex has to do with political freedom'. After all, the sexual choice for women had been 'between instinctive slavery and instinctive starvation'.[151] But Stella Browne felt this had held back women's sexual liberation. The 'incurably respectable tacticians of the old NUWSS and WSPU' had neglected 'intimate liberation'.[152] They also had to do battle with socialists, both reformist and revolutionary, who dismissed sexuality as irrelevant to politics.

This was partly a practical struggle, controversy in newspapers and journals, leafletting, speaking in meetings, raising questions in labour and trade-union meetings, speaking at conferences. But more than this they began to make a theory which connected the demands of birth control and abortion to the wider circumstances of women's sexual freedom. They derived support from other dissidents, particularly in Germany and Russia and the United States, who were challenging many of the assumptions of nineteenth century feminism and socialism. The new woman in the 1920s was extending her demands. She wanted the right to think on her own terms and the right to love on her own terms. She wanted economic freedom and motherhood, equality in politics, and equality in friendship. She wanted – quite simply – the right to be happy. It was of course all quite outrageous and there were no end of people to tell her so from the feminist, Mrs Fawcett, to the marxist 'Clete' and the social democrat, Ramsay MacDonald.

Stella Browne's scattered writings give a valuable picture of the range of political questioning and connecting among socialist feminists between the wars. Certainly they did not necessarily share all one another's views but many of their demands were the same.

The crux of Stella Browne's political thinking was the necessity for self-determination, for control. She did not think of reforms coming from above. She saw change being won from below. Just as Sanger before the First World War had been thinking about women's sexuality within a revolutionary socialist movement which was full of talk of direct action and rank and file workers' control, Browne's socialism carries echoes of 'Plebs' and of revolutionary syndicalism. She was unusual though in the British context during and after the First World War in trying to apply these ideas to sexual politics.

In her argument in *The Communist* in 1922, she asserted 'birth control for women is no less essential than workshop control and determination of the conditions of labour for men. . . . Birth control is woman's crucial effort at self-determination and at control of her own person and her own environment.'[153]

For Browne 'the communist case for birth control' was part of women's control over procreation and of a more general assertion of what she described as 'the work of liberation and human happiness implied by "creative revolution"'.[154] *Creative Revolution* was the title of a book written by Eden and Cedar Paul.

Like socialists and feminists in Greenwich Village and like Kollontai, Browne was searching for some means of understanding the creation of cultural forms and unsatisfied with a crude version of marxism which reduced Marx's writing on the dialectical relationship of consciousness, human social relations and the material world to 'economics'.

She expressed this in 1922 as 'understanding the importance of economic causation while recognising the increasing joint operation of psychical influences'.[155]

Though she never attempted a coherent theory of women's biological and social position and consciousness, she felt that giving some autonomy to these 'psychical influences' was connected to recognising the importance of sexual self-determination for women. 'No economic changes would give equality or self-determination to any woman unable to choose or refuse motherhood of her own free will.'[156] Women's material circumstances required change not only at work but in the ways in which a woman could experience love, give birth, and rear a child. Browne did not see a transformation in the conditions of reproduction as automatically following changes in the ownership and control of industrial production.

This insistence on women's control over reproduction had several political implications. It made her much more suspicious than many socialists and feminists were at that time of the neutrality of the state. In capitalist society, the state did not only express the interests of the ruling class, it was a masculine structure. It was therefore absurd to expect either equal rights or special protection for women from the state. She pointed out in her statement at the conference on birth control in 1922 how time, money and science could be devoted to finding destructive gases for warfare but not to invent a reliable contraceptive.[157] It was never safe for women 'to trust to the gratitude and justice of groups of men'.[158] Women would have to organise for their own interests. The idea that an oppressed group knew its own interests best had been an important element in early nineteenth century socialist feminism. It has had a somewhat uneasy existence in relation to the leninist concept of the party.

Contraception she saw as only one aspect of reproductive control. She had called for the legalisation of abortion as early as 1915 in her paper to the British Society for the Study of Sex Psychology, 'The Sexual Variety and Variability among Women'. She repeated this as a minority statement at the Fifth International Neo-Malthusian Conference in 1922.[159] The initial influence was probably Ellis. In Germany and the Soviet Union abortion was campaigned for and implemented by socialists in response to the conditions of war and revolution. Only later did support grow for contraception.[160]

Stella Browne found in her campaigning for birth control that working women came asking desperately for abortion. In her case, birth control convinced her that women must have the right to legal abortion as a condition of free motherhood and self-defined sexuality. She did not see abortion as a limited right – only for unmarried mothers or raped women for example. She wanted it to be equally available for all women. Indeed she argued at an International Conference on Sex Reform that, given the inadequacy of all known forms of contraception, early abortion could be erotically preferable for women.[161]

The 1861 Offences Against the Person Act made it illegal to commit an abortion. In the 1920s and 1930s between thirty and fifty men and women were sentenced each year for performing abortions. The punishment was imprisonment or penal servitude. Yet according to the midwives' report to the Interdepartmental Committee in 1938 women did not see it as a crime to abort yourself.[162] Perhaps they felt it was not a sin and assumed the law shared their views. The abortionist was frequently protected by the community – there was an often unspoken understanding among women of the terror of unwanted pregnancies: this was the reality as opposed to the idyll of motherhood – otherwise there would have been more convictions. At the foundation of the Abortion Law Reform Association in 1936 Mrs W.Williams from Leeds stated: 'In talking to a forewoman I know, she said she could tell the very point at which the women began to get nervous.'[163]

She knew herself 'of herbs and other curious things. In most villages one woman procures or tries to procure an abortion. There is a death and everyone knows who has done the abortion but none will tell.'[164]

From 1929 it became legal to abort if the mother's life was in danger. This provided a loophole but was more likely to favour middle-class patients who could persuade the doctor. At the ALRA meeting Nurse Daniels asserted that:

Poor women live under the spell of fear and they are always trying to get themselves right. Working women want abortion. Why should not the poor have it? Let the poor have what the rich have already got.[165]

Class injustice, maternal mortality and the persistent use of abortion despite its danger and illegality were arguments which convinced labour women in the Co-op Guild to support the demand for legal abortion. A report on the State of the Public Health in 1933 had estimated that one in seven pregnancies ended in abortion.

By the 1930s support for abortion as a means of ending the toll of suffering began to grow. But this was still regarded as a kind of favour not as a right. Stella Browne recognised the consequences of forced motherhood. Legal, safe, prompt abortion was necessary to abolish for ever, 'the trail of disease and crippling injuries, displacements, discharges, haemorrhages, inflammations'.[166] She went through the grounds given for limiting abortion carefully, showing how they would involve elaborate procedures of investigation, 'are we to install a dictaphone in every room, a moralist under every bed?'[167.]

Besides the practical problems of enforcement there was disagreement about the criteria of restriction which raised innumerable contradictory questions about who should have the right to grant or deny a woman control of her own body. Some people said it should be only for the unmarried, others just for the married. Abortion was sometimes seen as a way of helping women who were clearly victims of what was legally defined as rape or as incest. If abortion were to be legal in cases of rape alone, this would not protect women within marriage – Stella Browne pointed out that a husband could not legally rape his wife even if she resisted intercourse. Women ceased mysteriously to be victims and became the property of men:

Such suffering is an indictment of the whole social system that tolerates its infliction and is the ultimate expression of the view of women as vessels – of 'honour' and 'dishonour' as the case may be – for men's use and as automatic breeding machines. But these cases do not include the whole of the demand for women's right to abortion. This is based – as I see it – on justice rather than on pity.[168]

For Stella Browne abortion, like contraception, was essential for women's control of their own fertility. But other supporters of abortion did not see it in these terms. The politics of demanding abortion as a form of social hygiene to clear away the worse protuberances of sexism and exploitation in capitalism without any intention of changing fundamentally the conditions which caused them, could be incorporated within the conservative neo-Malthusian and eugenic idea of controlling reproduction from above. Stella Browne challenged this interpretation of reproductive control by her insistence on control by the woman herself:

Abortion must be the key to a new world for women, not a bulwark for things as they are, economically nor biologically. Abortion should not be either a perquisite of the legal wife only, or merely a last remedy against illegitimacy. It should be available for any woman, without insolent inquisitions, nor ruinous financial charges, nor tangles of red tape. For our bodies are our own.[169]

This assertion of women's choice remained a minority position. By the 1930s the political connections between workers' control over production and women's control over their bodies were becoming increasingly difficult to make. When ALRA gave evidence to Birkett's committee in 1937, they defended abortion mainly on the social grounds of reducing maternal deaths. Stella Browne demanded abortion as a right in an individual statement. Conservative opponents were glad to use the example of the Soviet Union against her. Abortion had become illegal there in 1936. Stella Browne replied that rather than being a humane measure which expressed women's interests, the change was a state measure, 'a reply to the intensive population policies of Germany and Japan and at the same time a propitiatory gesture towards the Catholics of Czecho-Slovakia and France'.[170]

She contrasted this with the reform of the Catalonian abortion law in December 1936 to include ethical, psychological and emotional stress as a reason for abortion. 'We have here a frank and emphatic recognition of the individuality of the woman and the quality of motherhood as distinct from mass production.'[171]

Birkett's committee refused to accept that women did not necessarily wish to have children. They stressed the danger of medical and psychological consequences from abortion. Stella Browne asked them:

What of the mental and emotional injuries of profoundly unwanted motherhood – injuries which have their lasting effects on the whole personality of the unwanted child and on its relationship to the mother.[172]

Birkett questioned her on the benefits of legal abortion in the Soviet Union and asked how she could possibly know it could be a safe operation without any medical professional knowledge. She answered,

I have – and I say this as a matter of public duty – the knowledge in my own person that if abortion were necessarily fatal or injurious, I should not now be before you.[173]

It was remarkably courageous for an unmarried woman in her fifties to reveal that she had had an abortion in the 1930s. Even in the 1960s ALRA campaigned for the 1967 Act on behalf of unfortunates, not from the experience of the women members themselves.

Stella Browne saw birth control and abortion as part of a wider transformation in the material circumstances and social relationships between men and women. She did not think that such changes would occur automatically with the ending of the capitalist mode of production but she also saw them as being inseparable from the making of a communist society. She formulated several basic preconditions for women's freedom in socialism. Women needed freedom to do any work for which they were fitted, protection for the child and child-bearing mother by the community along with the right to refuse motherhood and 'the freedom of sexual relationships from legal or economic coercion'.[174] She thought these new circumstances would help to dissolve the basis of 'patriarchal marriage'. She distinguished between a 'stereotyped monogamous formula' of sexual relationships and 'real monogamy' which 'will no longer be *stereotyped* as the one life-long and unvarying form of legally recognised expression for anything so infinitely variable and individual as the sexual impulse'.[175]

Socialism could provide a basis for a release of woman's 'sexual variability' by making new forms of relationship possible. She felt that under capitalism it was impossible for women to have real control over their reproductive capacity. She was aware that particular reforms around reproduction within capitalism would put the interests of the state before women's freedom to control their own sexual lives. Ironically, demands for better conditions for mothers could mean a more direct intervention of the state in the sphere of reproduction. For example, in reviewing Eleanor Rathbone's *The Disinherited Family*, she was critical of Rathbone's plan of handing over the children of unmarried parents to the Poor Law unless they married:

It is hoped that Maternity Endowment will never be used to bolster up stereotyped and outworn forms of marriage. Why should the child or children be made to suffer if its two progenitors refuse to turn a brief — though possibly worthwhile — illusion into a permanent incompatibility.[176]

Her radical commitment to making conditions in which men and women could develop infinitely varied sexual relations did not waver from her early paper to the British Society for Sex Psychology in 1915 to her writing on abortion in the 1930s. In 1915 she challenged the traditional view of women's sexual passivity, pointing out the absurdity of dividing women into two groups as the 'private sex property of one man' and the 'public sex property of all and sundry'.[177] She found a physiological explanation for her belief that women's sexual feelings varied considerably in Van de Velde's *Ideal Marriage* which she translated into German. Van de Velde argued for female genital diversity on the grounds that in some women 'the portio vaginalis and the cervix are as nervously sensitive and active as the clitoris'.[178]

It was consistent with her emphasis on women's determining their own sexuality that she should also challenge the denial of women's experience of their own biology. 'We lack a whole psychology of menstruation and need direct testimony from various types of women.'[179]

She also recognised that hidden female folk culture existed for women's complaints and that these remedies could still be useful. It was up to women doctors and scientists to bring 'their special feminine experience' to their studies and defy male interpretation of women's feelings.[180] 'There has grown up a masculine mythology suppressing and distorting all the facts of women's sexual and maternal emotions.'[181]

In connecting her demand for sexual liberation to a challenge of male culture, Stella Browne was very much part of the new feminism. Dora Russell in *The Right to be Happy* felt that legal equality or political freedom was illusory while, 'the whole mental picture which most people have of woman and her function, and which woman herself is still taught, is so false'.[182]

Russell stressed the 'stops and inhibitions implanted with childhood'.[183] Woman trying to assert her freedom in a world controlled by man was held back by the idea of femininity – itself a concept made by men:

It is as if a pianist were trying to perform in gloves or an actor to give an intimate and delicate performance in a mask. Our whole view of woman is still a mask between her and reality.[184]

Male domination and the cash nexus masked women's consciousness of herself and her sexuality. They also distorted male sexual feeling. Stella Browne maintained:

Most people are apt to under-rate the real strength of desire, and at the same time to exaggerate its indiscriminate facility. I submit that, though few women are absolutely monandrous, still fewer are really promiscuous. And I believe that much of the promiscuity of men is either a reaction from conditions of life and work, which a sane social order will abolish, or a response to organised commercial exploitation and therefore an artifical product.[185]

These questions were very much part of the current debate among feminists concerned about sexual questions. Apart from echoes of Havelock Ellis, Stella Browne's writing was undoubtedly influenced by these discussions. In 1917 she welcomed a book by Grete Meisel-Hess, *The Sexual Crisis: A Critique of our Sex Life*.[186] This book was evidently widely-read among feminists and socialists. It was extensively reviewed by Kollontai. Meisel-Hess made the same point as Browne about the effects of prostitution on men and Kollontai extended this into a statement about men's total response to women:

A man is not used to having to think about a woman's psychological and emotional experience. This means not only that he is unable to 'hear' a woman's soul, but with surprising naivety he ignores her physical experience during the sexual act.[187]

Meisel-Hess and Kollontai shared Carpenter's views on men's inability to express loving emotion, 'Modern man has no time to love.'[188]

But they were also both wary of the demands of intense love upon women, fearing they might be overwhelming because of women's subordination to men in love. With Stella Browne, they saw 'the great love' as the ideal but argued like her for much wider sexual choice for women in relationships which did not consume them totally. This would include what they called 'game-love' or 'loving friendships' in which the lovers could accept one another's autonomy. They saw the capacity for eroticism, of human 'potential for loving'[189] as a creative experience which could be developed.

Love cannot be forced or bought or even earned. To really *keep* anyone's love, much self-control is necessary, and much skill and care, and much instinctive respect for their individuality and one's own.[190]

Like Kollontai, Browne denied that the 'great love' should be regarded as the sole justification for women's sexual experience. On the contrary, women needed to recognise that we all had within us both the 'experimental love of variety and the permanent preference for one mate' but that women's sexual oppression required the particular acknowledgement of 'free experiment'.[191]

There were several aspects within Stella Browne's thinking though which acted as a brake on her radical commitment to creating the material conditions for sexual diversity. She followed Ellis, for instance, in distinguishing between congenital and artificial homosexuality. 'I repudiate all wish to slight or depreciate the love life of the real homosexual, but it cannot be advisable to force the growth of that habit in heterosexual people.'[192]

But even here she is aware that there is considerable complexity which makes it difficult to isolate the 'real' homosexual or the 'real' lesbian. She noted bisexuality among women:

Also many women of quite normally directed (heterosexual) inclinations, realise in mature life, when they have experienced passion, that the devoted admiration and friendship they felt for certain girl friends had a real, though perfectly unconscious, spark of desire in its exaltation and intensity, an unmistakable indefinable note, which was absolutely lacking in many equally sincere and lasting friendships.[193]

The emphasis on women's sexual liberation through relations with men rather than with women seems to have been a general feature of the sex reform movement in the early twentieth century, though many homosexual men were drawn into campaigns for sex reform. Indeed the conscious assertion of female sexuality may have contributed to a more defined cultural notion of the lesbian after the First World War. While there was a ban on discussion of any form of sexual feeling, lesbianism could inhabit a vague twilight world. Male homosexuality came to be seen in the late nineteenth century as the biological destiny of a social grouping rather than as a prohibited sexual practice. Edward Carpenter and Havelock Ellis had an important part in liberalising attitudes. However, the distinction they accepted between congenital and artificial homosexuality made it impossible to see homosexuality and lesbianism as aspects of a total span of sexual practices. They were to be tolerated rather than chosen.

Stella Browne also reproduces Carpenter and Ellis' ideas of fixed feminine characteristics. She sometimes assumes behaviour which could be socially created to be biologically determined. For example, she was convinced that women's sexuality was physiologically more diffused than men's and that this extended 'throughout the imaginative and emotional life'.[194] The acceptance of fixed gender characteristics contributed to the insistence within the new feminism on the importance of recognising a specific female condition and female culture.

Browne was aware of how the 'masculine mythology' about instinctive motherhood oppressed women, but she was liable herself to fall into sexual stereotypes of 'cold' and passionate natures, and her own mystical eugenics which asserted that children born in free love were somehow eugenically superior and inclining naturally to communism and feminism.

The notion of fixed characteristics meant that the new feminists did not challenge the total sexual division of labour between men and women. Stella Browne seems to have assumed that both child-bearing and child-rearing were organically women's work. This was a crucial weakness of new feminist politics which she did not question.

New feminist acknowledgement of a specifically female condition and culture was not enough to avoid a new and conservative role of natural womanhood. Women's material circumstances and social relations around the reproduction of the species had to be not only revealed but transformed.

It is easy too with historical hindsight to see that the shape of capitalism was itself changing so that some new feminist ideas about women's role could be accommodated as part of changes within the sexual division of labour, the structure of the family, attitudes to children, and the acceptance of sex without procreation. This accommodation was only possible because of the decline of feminism as a movement into a parliamentary lobby, a hardening both among non-marxist socialists and within the Communist Parties internationally which either excluded questions of the new life and personal liberation or placed them clearly on the sidelines. This accompanied a narrowing of political debate under Stalin in resisting first fascism and then the cold war. Sex reform persisted as a liberal or radical cause but both the feminist and revolutionary potential of sexual liberation seemed remote.[195]

This process of disconnection was not just external, it affected most profoundly the personal lives of those socialists who had dreamed, as Stella Browne said Edward Carpenter had, of that freedom which 'has to be won afresh every morning'.[196] Dora Russell has chronicled in *The Tamarisk Tree* how political and personal possibilities began to close with depression, fascism and war. Already, by the end of the

1920s, she felt terribly alone and began to feel her earlier personal and political hopes were irreconcilable:

There are periods in human history when, without apparent reason, at first imperceptibly, the movement in one direction goes into reverse. The change occurs not only in the economics and politics of the time but even in the motivation of individual lives . . . a mood, an atmosphere which affects the ideas and conduct of individuals, almost unknown to themselves.[197]

In such a context the vision of transformed relationships stretched painfully beyond the current definition of politics. With the economic crisis and the rise of fascism she sensed 'an unconscious polarisation of thought, for some back to the status quo, for others forward still to a forlorn hope for the future'.[198]

Stella Browne too undoubtedly experienced this change painfully in her own life. During the Second World War she moved to Liverpool to care for her sister who was ill. Stranded in this city with an old reputation of hostility to birth control and abortion, she sent frantic demands to ALRA for mass action when the tiny organisation could hardly pay their phone bill. This little, indomitable, unrespectable, fanatical foghorn of a feminist was still embarrassing the more staid of her fellow-campaigners. She died in 1955 aged 73 with her work, her politics and her ideas still disregarded.[199] She carried inside her so much passion against the sexual humiliation and cultural humbling of women in a world made by men:

What is this ban on abortion? It is a survival of the veiled face, of the barred window and the locked door, burning, branding, mutilation, stoning, of all the grip of ownership and superstition come down on woman, thousands of years ago.[200]

She had known the optimism of the rebels against Victorianism who imagined a new life breaking the integument of repression, international peace extending from love's body. As the years went by the hope must have grown heavy even for Stella Browne.

References to Section 1

1. Kathlyn Oliver, *The Freewoman*, 15 February 1912, p.252.
2. 'New Subscriber', *The Freewoman*, 22 February 1912, p.270.
3. Kathlyn Oliver, *The Freewoman*, 29 February 1912, p.290.
4. 'New Subscriber', *The Freewoman*, 7 March 1912, p.313.
5. 'New Subscriber', *The Freewoman*, 11 July 1912, p.158. I owe these references to Gloden Dallas.
6. Keith Hindell and Madeleine Simms, *Abortion Law Reformed*, London, Peter Owen 1971, p.58.
7. *The Freewoman*, 4 July 1912, p.135.
8. *The Malthusian*, 15 March 1914, p.20.
9. Quoted in Hindell and Simms, *op. cit.*, p.50.
10. David M.Kennedy, *Birth Control in America*, Yale U.P. 1970, pp.28–29.
11. F.W.Stella Browne, 'The Sexual Variety and Variability among Women and their Bearing upon Social Reconstruction', London, British Society for the Study of Sex Psychology 1917. See Appendix 1 below.
12. Peter Fryer, *The Birth Controllers*, London, Corgi 1967, p.215.
13. See Linda Gordon, *Woman's Body, Woman's Right. A Social History of Birth Control in America*, New York, Grossman 1976.
14. Kennedy, *op. cit.*, p.20.
15. Raymond Lee Muncy, *Sex and Marriage in Utopian Communities: Nineteenth Century America*, Baltimore, Penguin 1974, pp. 160–190.
16. Edward Carpenter, *Love's Coming of Age*, 10th ed London 1918, p.172.
17. Kennedy, *op. cit.*, pp.30–32. On Carpenter and Ellis, see Sheila Rowbotham and Jeffrey Weeks, *Socialism and the New Life: the Personal and Sexual Politics of Edward Carpenter and Havelock Ellis*, London, Pluto Press 1977.

18. Kennedy, *op. cit.*, p.33.

19. Stella Browne to Margaret Sanger, 7 September 1915.

20. Stella Browne to Margaret Sanger, 9 April, 18 April, 20 May 1917. I owe these references to Linda Gordon.

21. *The Malthusian*, 15 June 1920, p.42.

22. Guy Aldred, *No Traitor's Gait*, Glasgow, Strickland Press, Vol. 2, No.3, 1958, p.449. See also Sheila Rowbotham, *Hidden from History*, London, Pluto Press 1973, pp.100–102, 150–151.

23. Guy Aldred, 'The Religion and Economics of Sex Oppression', *Pamphlets for the Proletarian*, No. 2, 1907, pp.34–35. This pamphlet originated in a talk by Aldred to the SDF in Southwark in 1906 and was reprinted as *Socialism and Marriage* in 1914 with a dedication to Rose Witcop. See Guy Aldred, *Studies in Communism*, Glasgow, The World Library, No. 6, 1940, p.38.

24. Aldred, *No Traitor's Gait, op. cit.*, pp.447, 451–452.

25. For a discussion of changes in Sanger's political approach to birth control, see Linda Gordon, 'The Politics of Population: Birth Control and the Eugenics Movement', *Radical America*, Vol. 8, No. 4, July–August 1974, pp.64–66. A more extensive study of this topic is included in Gordon, *Woman's Body, Woman's Right, op. cit.*

26. See Eden and Cedar Paul (eds), *Population and Birth Control. A Symposium*, New York 1917, pp.121, 149 and 167; Bernard Semmel, *Imperialism and Social Reform*, London, Allen & Unwin 1960, pp.64–82. See also Gordon, 'The Politics of Population', *op. cit.*

27. Eden Paul, 'The Sexual Life of the Child', London, British Society for the Study of Sex Psychology 1921, and Workers' Suffrage Federation, *Minutes*, 9 December 1917, Institute of Social History, Amsterdam.

28. Stella Browne to Margaret Sanger, 20 May 1917. I owe this reference to Linda Gordon.

29. F.W.Stella Browne, 'Women and Birth Control' in Eden and Cedar Paul (eds) *Population and Birth Control, op. cit.*, p.251.

30. Jane Lewis, 'Beyond Suffrage, English Feminism during the 1920s', *The Maryland Historian*, Vol. VI, Spring 1975, p.8.

31. For a fuller analysis of this question in the context of the contemporary women's movement, see Barbara Taylor, 'Our Labour and Our Power', *Red Rag*, No. 10.

References to Section 2

32. Peter Fryer, *The Birth Controllers*, *op. cit.*, pp.286–288. Fryer also describes the utopian socialist writings on birth control. See also Angus McLaren, 'Contraception and the Working Classes', *Comparative Studies in Society and History*, Vol. 18, No. 2, April 1976, pp.236 and 251.

33. Aldred, *No Traitor's Gait*, *op. cit.*, p.453.

34. *ibid.*, p.454.

35. *The Malthusian*, 15 February and 15 March 1919.

36. *The Times*, 13 April 1919.

37. *The Sunday Chronicle*, 20 April 1919.

38. *The Times*, 26 August 1918.

39. F.W.Stella Browne, 'Birth Control in Taff Vale. A Socialist Synthesis', *The New Generation*, October 1923, p.116.

40. 'Clete', 'Birth Control', *The Communist*, 5 August 1922.

41. *ibid.*

42. *ibid.*, 19 August 1922.

43. *ibid.*, 26 August 1922.

44. *ibid.*

45. *ibid.*

46. Alice Waters, Feminism and the Marxist Movement', *International Socialist Review*, October 1972. On this discussion generally in the Soviet Union, see Sheila Rowbotham, *Women, Resistance and Revolution*, London, Allen Lane 1973, pp.134–168. On the Bolsheviks' suspicion of autonomous women's organisation, see Anne Bobroff, 'The Bolsheviks and Working Women, 1905–20', *Radical America*, Vol. 10, No. 3, May–June 1976.

47. *Report on Organisation Presented by the Party Commission to the Annual Conference of the C.P.G.B.*, 7 October 1922, p.46.

48. Stella Browne, 'The Feminine Aspect of Birth Control', *Report of the Fifth International Neo-Malthusian and Birth-Control Conference*, 11–14 July 1922, p.43.

49. *The New Generation*, October 1922, p.1.

50. *The New Generation*, November 1922, p.3.

51. *ibid.*

52. *ibid.*

53. Fryer, *op. cit.*, p.359.

54. F.W.Stella Browne, 'The Women's Question', *The Communist*, 11 March 1922.

55. 'Norseman', *The New Generation*, February 1924, p.21.

56. See Henry Pelling, *The British Communist Party*, London, Black 1958, pp.15–32 and Hugo Dewar, *Communist Politics in Britain*, London, Pluto Press 1976, pp.21–36.

57. F.W.Stella Browne, 'Birth Control in Taff Vale', *The New Generation*, October 1923, p.116.

58. *ibid.*

59. *ibid.*

60. F.W.Stella Browne, 'My Tour in Monmouthshire', *The New Generation*, January 1924, p.9.

61. Quoted in Fryer, *The Birth Controllers*, p.287.

62. Drusilla Modjeska, 'Dora Russell, A Quest for Liberty and Love', *Spare Rib*, No. 54 [1977], p.34.

63. Dora Russell, 'The Long Campaign', *New Humanist*, December 1974, p.260.

64. Quoted in Edith How-Martyn and Mary Breed, *The Birth Control Movement in England*, London, John Bale 1930, p.26.

65. Russell, 'The Long Campaign', *op. cit.*, p.260.

66. Dora Russell, *The Tamarisk Tree. My Quest for Liberty and Love*, London, Elek 1975, p.174.

67. Browne, 'The Feminine Aspect of Birth Control', *op. cit.*, p.42. Hindell and Simms, *Abortion Law Reformed*, *op cit.*, pp.58–59, and Abortion Law Reform Association, London 1936, pp.14–15 (pamphlet).

68. See Rowbotham, *Hidden from History*, *op. cit.*, p.156.

69. Dorothy Jewson, 'The Labour Party Conference and Birth Control', *The New Generation*, November 1925, p.127.

70. *ibid.*

71. Dora Russell, *Hypatia*, London, Norwood 1925, pp.4–5.

72. 'Mrs Thurtle's Protest', *The New Generation*, April 1926, p.40.

73. Stella Browne, 'Women Workers Who Think', *The New Generation*, September 1922, p.6.

74. Stella Browne, 'Plain Words to the Labour Party', *The New Generation*, February 1927, p.19. Stella Browne, 'Victory or Compromise' *The New Generation*, April 1927, p.39. See Fryer, *op. cit.*, pp.294–296, on the Catholic opposition to birth control.

75. 'Stella Browne at Feltham, Middlesex', *The New Generation*, July 1924, p.81.

76. Browne, *The New Generation*, February 1927, p.14.

77. Browne, *The New Generation*, November 1926, p.112.

78. Quoted in Jewson, *The New Generation*, November 1925, p.127.

79. Modjeska, *op. cit.*, p.34.

80. Gladstone, quoted in Andrew Rosen, *Rise Up Women*, London 1974, p.10.

81. Ramsay MacDonald, quoted in Mary Agnes Hamilton, *J. Ramsay MacDonald*, London 1929, p.39.

82. *The Freewoman*, 11 January 1912, p.151.

83. F.W.Stella Browne, 'Progress of the Movement', *The New Generation*, May 1927, p.52.

84. Modjeska, *op. cit.*, pp. 34–35.

85. Russell, *The Tamarisk Tree*, *op. cit.*, p.170.

86. Dora Russell to Sheila Rowbotham.

87. Hannah Mitchell, *The Hard Way Up*, London, Faber 1968, p.102.

88. Gloden Dallas and Suzie Fleming, 'Jessie', interview with Jessie Stephen, *Spare Rib*, No. 32, p.13.

89. See Lewis, 'Beyond Suffrage, English Feminism in the 1920s', *The Maryland Historian*, Vol. VI, Spring 1975, pp.1–17.

90. See Abortion Law Reform Association, *op. cit.*, 1936, and Diana Gittins, 'Married Life and Birth Control between the Wars', *Oral History*, Vol. 3, No. 2, p.53. On the arguments used by ALRA after the Second World War, see Victoria Greenwood and Jock Young, *Abortion in Demand*, London, Pluto Press 1976, pp.74–86 and pp.116–117. For discussion of the implications of changes in child bearing and housework as part of the total pattern of reproduction since the 1930s, see Political Economy of Women Group, *Women, the State and Reproduction since the 1930s, On the Political Economy of Women*, CSE Pamphlet, No. 2, London, Stage 1 1976, pp.17–33, and Jean Gardiner, 'A Case Study in Social Change: Women in Society, Reform or Revolution?' The Open University, Units 31–32, 1976, pp.63–66.

References to Section 3

91. For information about neo-Malthusian and eugenic pressure among birth controllers I am grateful to Jane Lewis, 'The English Birth Control

Movement, Neo-Malthusianism to Constructive Birth Control' (un-published paper).

92. See Rowbotham, *Hidden from History*, *op. cit.*, pp.144–145.

93. Russell, 'The Long Campaign', *op. cit.*, p.260.

94. Gittins, *op. cit.*, p.53.

95. I am grateful to Linda Gordon for this point. On methods and the dissemination of information see Gittins, *op. cit.*

96. Dallas and Fleming, *op. cit.*, p.13.

97. Norman E. Hines, 'English Birth Control Clinics', *Eugenics Review*, Vol. 59, No. 4, 1928, p.159.

98. Ministry of Health, *Evidence before the Interdepartmental Committee on Abortion* (mh 71/18) 1938; in Public Record Office.

99. David Widgery, 'Abortion: The Pioneers', *International Socialism*, No. 80, p.7.

100. Ministry of Health, *Evidence before the Interdepartmental Committee on Abortion*, *op. cit.*

101. *37th Annual Report of the Malthusian League*, 31 March 1915, p.5. See also Fryer, *op. cit.*, pp.262–265.

102. *The Malthusian*, 15 October 1920, p.74.

103. Fryer, *op. cit.*, pp.253–254.

104. *ibid.*, p.279.

105. *The New Generation*, September 1922, p.6.

106. *The New Generation*, July 1922, p.14, and *The Malthusian*, 15 October 1920, p.70.

107. *The New Generation*, June 1925, p.62.

108. *The New Generation*, September 1922, p.6.

109. *ibid.*

110. *ibid.*

111. Fryer, *op. cit.*, pp.282–283. On Glasgow see Stella Browne, 'Progress of the Movement', *The New Generation*, May 1927, p.52.

112. Hines, 'English Birth Control Clinics', *op. cit.*, pp.157–158.

113. Fryer, *op. cit.*, p.281.

114. *The New Generation*, January 1923, pp.1–3.

115. Russell, 'The Long Campaign', *op. cit.*, p.260.

116. *The New Generation*, April 1923, p.42.

117. Aldred, *No Traitor's Gait*, *op. cit.*, Vol. 3, No. 1, 1963, pp.440–442.

118. Russell, 'The Long Campaign', *op. cit.*, p.260.

119. *The New Generation*, April 1923, p.50.

120. *ibid.* April 1923, p.50; June 1923, p.11; September 1923, p.106; October 1923, p.31; November 1923, p.138.

121. *ibid.*, November 1923, p.138.

122. *ibid.*, October 1924, p.114.

123. *ibid.*, October 1923, p.31.

124. Stella Browne, 'My Tour in Monmouthshire', *The New Generation*, January 1924, p.8.

125. *The New Generation*, March 1924, p.29; February 1924, p.19; May 1924, p.51; June 1924, p.69; July 1924, p.73.

126. *ibid.*, June 1924, p.63.

127. *ibid.*

128. *ibid.*, p.64.

129. *ibid.*

130. *ibid.*, May 1924, p.51.

131. *ibid.*, October 1924, p.109.

132. *ibid.*, October 1924, p.104.

133. Russell, *The Tamarisk Tree, op. cit.*, p.174.

134. Stella Browne, 'The Labour Party Conference', *The New Generation*, November 1924, p.124.

135. *ibid.*

136. Russell, *The Tamarisk Tree, op. cit.*, p.172.

137. Dorothy Jewson, 'The Labour Party Conference and Birth Control', *The New Generation*, November 1925, p.127.

138. *The New Generation*, November 1925, p.123.

139. Beatrice McCabe, 'Our Tour', *The New Generation*, January 1926, p.3.

140. *The New Generation*, March 1926, p.25. See also Fryer, *op. cit.*, p.290.

141. Russell, *The Tamarisk Tree, op. cit.*, p.184.

142. *ibid.*

143. Stella Browne, 'Labour Demands Birth Control', *The New Generation*, November 1926, pp.111–112.

144. Fryer, *op. cit.*, p.291.

145. *ibid.*, p.292.

146. Stella Browne, 'How the Fight Goes', *The New Generation*, August 1930, p.88.

References to Section 4

147. F.W.Stella Browne, 'Women and Birth Control', In Eden and Cedar Paul (eds), *op. cit.*, p.247.

148. F.W.Stella Browne, 'The Women's Question', *The Communist*, 11 March 1922.

149. F.W.Stella Browne, 'Women and Birth Control', in Eden and Cedar Paul (eds), *op. cit.*, pp.248–249.

150. *The New Generation*, July 1922, p.14.

151. Dora Russell, *The Right to be Happy*, London 1927, pp.147–148.

152. *The New Generation*, February 1925, p.23.

153. Stella Browne, letter to *The Communist*, 19 August 1922.

154. *The New Generation*, November 1922, p.3.

155. *ibid.*

156. *ibid.* Browne thought Kollontai had a 'more intimate psychological perception' than many marxists (*The New Generation*, April 1922, p.4). On feminism in Greenwich Village, see June Sochen, *Movers and Shakers, the New Woman in Greenwich Village 1910–1920*, New York 1972.

157. Browne, 'The Feminine Aspect of Birth\Control', *op. cit.*, p.41.

158. Browne, 'Women and Birth Control', in Eden and Cedar Paul (eds), *op. cit.*, p.249.

159. F.W.Stella Browne, 'The Sexual Variety and Variability among Women and their bearing upon Social Reconstruction', London, British Society of Sex Psychology 1917, pp.13–14. (See Appendix 1 below, p.87.)

160. *The New Generation*, June 1923, p.66. For an account of the abortion campaign in Germany, see 'Communist Women in Other Lands', *The Communist*, 15 July 1922.

161. F.W.Stella Browne, 'The Right to Abortion', in Stella Browne, A.M.Ludovici, Harry Roberts, *Abortion*, p.44, London, Allen & Unwin 1935. (see Appendix 2 below pp.107–124.)

162. See Interdepartmental Committee on Abortion, 1938.

163. Abortion Law Reform Association, *op. cit.*, 1936, p.18.

164. *ibid.*

165. *ibid.*, p.19.

166. Browne, 'The Right to Abortion', *op. cit.*, p.33.

167. *ibid.*, p.39.

168. *ibid.*, p.29.

169. *ibid.*, p.31.

170. Stella Browne, Evidence to Interdepartmental Committee on Abortion, 1938, *op. cit.*

171. *ibid.*

172. *ibid.*

173. *ibid.*

174. Stella Browne, 'The Women's Question', *The Communist*, 11 March 1922.

175. Browne, 'The Feminine Aspect of Birth Control', *op. cit.*, p.41.

176. *The New Generation*, February 1925, p.22.

177. Browne, 'The Sexual Variety and Variability among Women', *op. cit.*, p.4. (See Appendix 1 below p.92.)

178. Browne, 'The Right to Abortion', *op. cit.*, p.181.

179. Browne, 'The Sexual Variety and Variability among Women', *op. cit.*, p.9. (See Appendix 1 below p.99.)

180. Browne, 'Women and Birth Control', in Eden and Cedar Paul (eds), *Population and Birth Control*, *op. cit.*, p.252.

181. *ibid.* p.4.

182. Russell, *The Right to be Happy*, *op. cit.*, p.142.

183. *ibid.*, p.148.

184. *ibid.*

185. Browne, 'The Sexual Variety and Variability among Women', *op. cit.*, p.6. (See Appendix 1 below, p.94.)

186. *The Malthusian*, 15 May 1917.

187. See Alexandra Kollontai, *Sexual Relations and the Class Struggle, Love and the New Morality*, Bristol, Falling Wall Press 1972, p.19 (1st ed 1919).

188. *ibid.*, p.20.

189. *ibid.*, p.22.

190. Browne, 'The Sexual Variety and Variability among Women', *op. cit.*, p.7. (See Appendix 1 below, pp.95–96.)

191. *ibid.*, p.7.

192. *ibid.*, p.12.

193. *ibid.*

194. *ibid.*, p.8.

195. This kind of question is only just beginning to be asked of the history of political organisations. Local branch reality may have been different.

For example, Zelda Curtis remembers reading Ellis in her Communist Party branch in the 'thirties, conscious of being very advanced. Also in the mid 'thirties in Battersea, as a new woman member, Daphne Morgan remembers being whisked off to the birth control clinic by the Branch Secretary, where she was fitted up with a diaphragm and put on the committee of the clinic.

196. Quoted in Stella Browne, 'Liberty and Democracy', *The Birth Control Review*, February 1921, Vol. 2.

197. Russell, *The Tamarisk Tree*, p.216.

198. *ibid.*

199. See Keith Hindell and Madeleine Simms, *Abortion Law Reformed*, pp.58–59, 61 and Keith Hindell, 'Stella Browne and Janet Chance', *The Listener*, 29 June 1972, pp.851–858.

200. Abortion Law Reform Association, *op. cit.*, 1936, p.28.

Appendix 1
'The Sexual Variety and Variability among Women'
by F.W.Stella Browne
Introduced by Sheila Rowbotham

Stella Browne's paper on 'The Sexual Variety and Variability among Women' was first read at a meeting of the British Society for the Study of Sex Psychology on 14 October 1915. It was published two years later.

The Society for the Study of Sex Psychology which was formed during the First World War brought together the older sexual radicals who had rebelled against Victorian middle-class morality and the younger generation for whom the old world was being overturned by the war. Important influences within the Society were Laurence Housman who had supported women's suffrage, Edward Carpenter the author of *Love's Coming of Age*, Havelock Ellis, pioneer writer on the psychology of sex, and Eden Paul, a socialist involved in the Malthusian League and interested in eugenics.

The Society aimed proudly:

to question things that have not been questioned before . . . we mean to push our enquiry on the basis of men and women working fearlessly and frankly together over territory that is really common to both, but which hitherto has been ridiculously cut up, separated and divided.

They believed, 'that nothing concerning sex can be rightly dealt with by one sex deciding and acting alone, and that in consequence of decisions so formed and so acted upon society is suffering today'.

Ellis and Carpenter were early influences on Stella Browne's ideas about sex and she mentions them in her correspondence with Margaret Sanger as well as Housman. The impact of Ellis is evident in 'The Sexual Variety and Variability among Women' paper. But her connection to Eden Paul was also to be very significant in introducing her to contemporary European thinking about sexuality and the liberation of women. Before the First World War Eden Paul had read or translated not only Krafft Ebing, but some of Freud's works as well as writers who are forgotten now; Heinrich Kisch's *The Sexual Life of Women*; Ivan Bloch's *The Sexual Life of Our Time*; and Grete Meisel-Hess's *The Sexual Crisis*.

Though all members of the society for the Study of Sex Psychology did not agree with Stella Browne's ideas about women's sexuality and disclaimed responsibility for the paper, Eden Paul seems to have been in sympathy with her insistence on the hold of men's experience of sex over the understanding of women's psychology. In 1921 he commented in a paper to the Society on *The Sexual Life of the Child*, 'We are too much dependent upon males for our knowledge of sex life.' They were also brought together by their activity in the birth control movement.

It is not surprising if the style of sexual discussion in Stella Browne's paper appears somewhat dated now. Its context is still that of the feminist paper *The Freewoman* with its conscious commitment to the creation of a new morality. There are also similarities to Kollontai's *The New Morality and the Working Class* which was published in 1919 in the Soviet Union and translated into German the following year. Some of the preoccupations are with contemporary debates among feminists about the 'great love' – a theme which fascinated Kollontai. Browne has a tendency to invent types of women echoing the sex psychology of Carpenter and Ellis and this influences her attitude towards lesbianism.

Despite this specific historical context, there is still also a very modern relevance in what she says about love and women's sexual feelings. She was aware above all of the complexity of desires buried by a culture which denied them. She wanted to create a society in which women could express and realise their sexuality and this was to bring her into opposition to male domination and to the sexual oppression general in capitalism. She was aware of the specific ignorances about women's bodies, for example menstruation and the menopause and the need to base female health care on the 'direct testimony' of women themselves rather than men's theories of what women 'ought' to be experiencing. She saw birth control and abortion as crucial aspects of this general challenge to men's hold over women's sexual life and consciousness.

Stella Browne's attempt to discuss women's sexuality in relation to economic and social change raises a theoretical problem which still faces socialists and feminists; how to connect our innermost sexual feelings to the more public and external social transformation which we seek? Kollontai was similarly concerned with this relationship between the personal and political. Indeed she felt its solution was made even more vital by the circumstances of the Russian Revolution. Theoretically though both Kollontai and Browne tend to detach the inner consciousness or 'psyche' from the outer world of 'economics'. It seems that there was no explicit theory about the relations of reproduction; procreation, child rearing and women's domestic labour in the family and production for the cash nexus, or any theory about the total division of labour between the sexes as a historical process which could begin to penetrate this separation of sexual consciousness from material existence. Socialist feminists in this period *described* particular aspects of women's oppression with great perception, but they rarely analysed their inter-relationship. Stella Browne was remarkable in making the connection between control over the means of production and women's control over procreation in the early 1920s but the implications of feminism for revolutionary socialism could not be really developed.

The Sexual Variety and Variability among Women and their Bearing upon Social Reconstruction
by F. W. Stella Browne

Perhaps I had better preface what I have to say, by stating my point of view on some essential subjects.

I do not think that any intelligent, humane and self-respecting attitude towards sex is generally possible, without great economic changes; and a responsible education in the laws of sex, and a much wider co-operation and companionship between men and women, wholly apart from erotic relations, are equally necessary.

I am utterly opposed to the 'double standard'; but I believe the 'double standard' is an integral part of a certain social order: to repudiate that standard, while upholding and accepting the social order, seems to me absurd.

Finally: I do not accept traditional platitudes: especially not that doctrine of the uncleanness of sex, insisted on by the Christian – or as it should be called, the Pauline – superstition.

Now what are the assumptions underlying the conventional view of women's sexuality?

1. The denial, first of all, of any strong, spontaneous, discriminating, – note these qualifications – sex impulse in women.

2. The division of women into two arbitrary classes,

corresponding to no psychological or ethical individual differences: as

(*a*) The prospective or actual private sex property of one man.

(*b*) The public sex property of all and sundry.

3. The over-rating, which amounts sometimes to a sadistic fetishism, of one manifestation of sex and one characteristic.

Hence the belief that the majority of women, those not belonging to the prostitute class, feel neither curiosity, nor desire on these matters, while they are maidens. And that when their sexual life has begun, its physical side is quite subordinate, and merely a *response* to their husbands.

Also that no woman who has any principle or any fastidiousness, can be physically attracted to more than one man; in the words of the thousand-fold repeated cliché: 'Woman is instinctively monogamous, while man is polygamous.'

The upholders of this doctrine do not propose to dispense with the promiscuously polyandrous class of women who are the necessary concomitants of a system of patriarchal marriage – especially monogamous marriage; and of compulsory chastity for most women before marriage. Yet this class of women is in no State adequately protected, least of all in the States which profess Christianity. It is hoped that the whole question of the status and psychology of the prostitute will be very carefully studied. I will only suggest here, that the experience of Eastern civilisations, frankly and systematically patriarchal for thousands of years, tends to show that polygamy legally recognised, is not in itself any remedy against prostitution. That remedy lies far deeper.

I believe that the conventional estimate of women's sexual apathy and instinctive monandry is not true. Any man of exceptional vitality and attractions knows it is not true. So does any man of exceptional intelligence and sensitiveness. So does any observant traveller, acquainted with human habits under conditions which do not foster artificial ignorance and dependence in women. The history of any time in which women − generally of course, only a small percentage of women in the ruling class − were given any freedom and scope, proves that this theory is not true: the Empresses and patrician ladies of Rome, the Renaissance princesses and courtesans, Christine of Sweden, the Russian Tzaritzas, Elizabeth Petrovna and Catherine the Great, and the Frenchwomen who are so intimately a part of seventeenth and eighteenth century culture.

Most experienced lawyers and doctors will admit privately, at least, that this theory is not true. Finally, women are beginning to say so themselves.

The sexual emotion in women is not, taking it broadly, weaker than in men. But it has an enormously wider range of variation; and much greater diffusion, both in desire and pleasure, all through women's organisms. And thirdly, arising from these two characteristics of variability and diffusion, it is extremely liable to aberrations and perversions, which, I believe, under constant social and religious repression of normal satisfaction, have often developed to a pathological extent, while sometimes remaining almost entirely subconscious.

The variability of the sexual emotion in women is absolutely basic and primary. It can never be expressed or satisfied by either patriarchal marriage or prostitution. It is found in the same woman as between different times, and in different individuals. This is the cause of much cant and bitterness between women, for there is a considerable and pretty steady percentage of cold natures, who may yet be very efficient and able and very attractive to men. These cold women generally have a perfect mania for *prohibition* as a solution for all ills. But surely, we do not want the new world to be built up only by women who have long ago forgotten what sex means, or who have never experienced strong sexual emotions, and regard them as a sign of grossness or decadence.

I think no one who knows the 'personnel' of many social reform movements, can doubt that this is a very real danger. Persons of cold temperament have special aptitudes for much valuable work: they have their peculiar excellences, their precious achievements. But they must not alone make the laws for more ardent natures.

And the greatest drawback of the sexually frigid woman is the ease with which her coldness adapts itself to venality and vulgarity, whether conventionally sanctioned or not.

It is this variety and variability of the sexual impulse among women, which would militate against any real promiscuity, if women were all economically secure and free to follow their own instincts, and to control their maternal function by the knowledge of contraceptives (a most important part of women's real emancipation). Most people are apt to under-rate the real strength of desire, and at the same time, to exaggerate its indiscriminate facility. I submit that, though few women are absolutely monandrous, still fewer are really promiscuous. And I believe that much of the promiscuity of men is either a reaction from conditions of life and work, which a sane social order will abolish, or a response to organised commercial exploitation, and therefore an artificial product. In a social order where women were not tempted for bread and butter, and any of the 'jam' of life, to exploit the desires of men, it would soon become apparent that the sexual instinct is selective. The most ardent natures, if they are not insane or suffering from prolonged sexual starvation, have their cool quiescent times; and I think no woman who has had the inestimable happiness and interest of real friendship with men, can doubt that it may exist without any conscious sexual desire. Much of the unhealthiness of sexual conditions at present, is due to the habit of segregating the sexes in childhood and partly in latter life, and making them into 'alien enemies' to one another. Some measure of co-education and a much wider professional and administrative co-operation will clarify our views, and induce a more generous and human tone.

One form of shibboleth, which has superseded the shibboleths of the virtue of compulsory abstinence, and the duty of unwilling surrender in marriage, among some advanced women, is the shibboleth of the 'great love'. Let me not be mistaken here. I believe the great love exists, and that is the greatest gift of whatever gods may be, to humanity. But I do not believe that the great love is the sole justification of sexual experience. Most natures are not capable of it. They have not strong and sure enough intuitive instinct. They are not sufficiently evolved. The great love can no more be demanded to order than the emotion which it most of all resembles – an ecstatic religious faith. Moreover, our social system seems designed expressly to thwart and stifle it. Women must learn to recognise that all persons are not on the same plane, psychically or physiologically. They might also profitably turn their efforts towards removing the barriers, which at present generally doom a great love to slow frustration or sudden catastrophe.

Jealousy, both physical and psychic, will always be the shadow of passionate love, and even of most strong affection. But it is unnecessary and barbarous to consecrate jealousy in one, and only one, special set of circumstances. Love cannot be forced, or bought, or even earned. To really *keep* anyone's love, much self-control is necessary, and much skill and care, and much instinctive respect for their individuality and one's own. It should be recognised that the art of attracting and satisfying desire is a part of refined civilisation, and not necessarily mercenary or degrading in any way. But women must demand more of life – and give more to it. Let them set their own requirements, and boldly claim a share of life and erotic experience, as perfectly consistent with their own self-respect – and realise also, that love can only be a part of life, and sometimes a small part, to any man with big work to do in the world. Both the experimental love of variety and the permanent preference for one mate are inherent in all human beings. And in women there is a special need for recognising free experiment. First love is generally almost entirely an illusion, and many women have ruined their lives, because an illusion was made permanent and petrified by marriage. General early marriage, even if possible under present conditions, does not solve the sex question. Women's erotic experiments will probably be always less numerous than men's, and include more 'amitiés amoureuses'; but they are an integral part of life.

The very consciousness of being desired, even by a man who does not overwhelmingly attract her (provided he is not positively repellent), is a tonic to most women: and the sexual relation, when happy and harmonious, vivifies a woman's brain, develops her character, and trebles her vitality. The comparative intellectual barrenness of woman is just as much due to the nervous corrosion and mental torpor, caused by prolonged sexual repression, as to the lack of education and the exclusion from prominent and responsible positions.

Even the great love, *in women as in men*, by no means always excludes lesser attractions and intimacies, which may run the whole gamut from sentiment and camaraderie to the frankly physical, yet remain totally distinct from the dominant passion. I allude, of course, to genuine, even if transitory, impulses, not to commercial transactions for pearls or cheques or livelihood. Indeed, I think this is the test of the great love, that any minor episode seems to heighten one's desire for, and pleasure in, it.

Diffusion of the sexual emotions in women is not merely physiological: it extends throughout the imaginative and emotional life. It helps the transmutation of desire into religious devotion, charity, musical and poetic appreciation, etc. It is the basis of inherent modesty, as contrasted with conventional modesty. It is the perpetual contradiction of the ecclesiastical view of sex, as a somewhat low and uncleanly prelude to the act of procreation. This diffusion is the main cause of the greater slowness and complexity of the sexual processes in women. Finally it makes the traditional masculine over-estimate of, and insistence on anatomical virginity, the most ridiculous superstition in the world. Even if we consider sexual ignorance and intactitude as a woman's highest charm, and virtue – the unruptured hymen is no guarantee of this ignorance and intactitude. It may co-exist with the most varied and even perverted sex experience. Virginity will always have a value and charm for men, and consequently it will always be a source of keen pleasure to women, to be able to give this gift to their beloved. But the woman whose virginity is her chief charm, has very little intelligence, vitality or passion: even very little character. And in any case this anatomical accident is something quite distinct from modesty, or from that instinctive discrimination and proud self-control which alone deserve the name chastity.

The diffused sexuality of women, again, is the enemy of all very abrupt transformations and transitions: no social order which took this fact adequately into consideration, could tolerate the present forms of marriage, with the outrage on decency and freedom alike involved in the idea of 'conjugal rights'.

No woman has been given her full share of the beauty and the joy of life, who has not been very gradually and skilfully initiated into the sexual relation. Marcel Prévost's affected reprobation of the 'demi-vièrge' is equally stupid and cruel. A really satisfactory lover must have insight and intuition as well as virility and passion: he must respect his mate's individuality, and be able to exercise an iron self-control: his own enjoyment will be all the keener in the end. How far do education and social institutions, not to speak of the mawkish cant miscalled religion, help to develop this respect and self-control?

The existence of prostitution is a great wrong to women and love, in subtle as well as in obvious ways: it not only debases the whole view of sex, but − combined with the abuse of alcohol − it favours a mechanical facility of the sexual process in men, which increases the natural difficulty due to women's slowness in reaching complete gratification, thus causing disappointment and disharmony.

Women vary greatly in respect of the periodic function. Here I can only briefly point out the importance of sex education, in helping to establish this function in a healthy manner and minimising nervous disturbances. Many girls suffer for years, and form bitter and distorted views of life, as a result of the neglect which allowed them to meet the shock of puberty unprepared, or with only a revoltingly crude, inadequate warning. In my opinion, in the social order for which some of us hope and work, provision will have to be made for women's periodic changes; menstruation and the menopause, must be recognised and 'allowed for', as well as gestation and child-birth. I know that many experienced medical women, whose knowledge and judgment I respect, believe that under fair and healthy conditions, menstruation will gradually become almost negligible. I cannot think so; though, certainly, it has been made needlessly painful and debilitating, and one of the chief agents in aggravating its symptoms and effects, has been persistent sexual repression. I believe most women after they have formed sexual relations, find that the periodic pain and weakness decrease considerably; *even, be it noted, when sexual gratification stops short of complete intercourse.* Of course the average woman, is not given time to benefit by this new experience before she has to face the changes and risks of pregnancy.

We lack a whole psychology of menstruation, and need direct testimony from *various types* of women. Disturbances of the function may occur as the result of sexual excitement, whether satisfied or not; also of almost any unusual physical exertion or emotional excitement, as well as from purely physiological causes. Also among 'civilised' women, it is not invariably accompanied by definite sexual desire, though the two tend to be correlated, and some women are at their maximum of strength and efficiency just before the period: others again, though they may suffer a good deal while menstruating, feel an indescribable access of general energy and well-being in the week, or fortnight, afterwards. I suggest to you, that menstruation may *have some important psychophysical purpose, quite apart from ovulation*, which we do not yet understand; and that definite investigations be made, as to whether certain phenomena of menstruation, and certain types of menstrual activity, e.g. the three or five days' period – are correlated with certain special mental, temperamental and constitutional qualities.

The repressed sex-impulse in women often breaks out

irresistibly at the change of life, sometimes undermining sanity and control, throughout the remaining years. The happy memories and influences of a complete and active life, will always be a great safeguard through the critical years, to a wise, healthy, kindly old age. The suggestion has been made by Dr Drysdale, in the *Malthusian* for May 1915, that the period of effective sexual life may be much extended by rational hygienic habits. Shortly after Dr Drysdale's suggestion, Dr Mary Scharlieb, in a paper quoted by the *British Medical Journal*, independently made the statement that the menopause now occurred, on the average, four or five years later than two generations ago. Certainly, birth-control is more widely practised than in our grandmothers' time – I hope and believe also, that there is less involuntary abstinence and repression among women now, than then, though there is room for immense advance along both lines of progress!

The education of women together with the complexity of their emotional life, and their special physiology, help to stimulate sexual aberrations to a degree which is not generally realised; but it is none the less important and injurious. I wish particularly to make this point clear. Of course, normal sexuality includes the beginnings of most abnormal instincts. The pleasure in either inflicting a certain degree of pain on the beloved one, or suffering a certain degree of pain from them, is almost inextricably a part of desire. So are certain forms of fetishism, as Mr Housman so acutely insisted in his introductory paper. We are learning to recognise congenital inversion as a vital and very often valuable factor in civilisation, subject of course, to the same restraints as to public order and propriety, freedom of consent, and the protection of the immature, as normal heterosexual desire. Also a certain amount of self-excitement, and solitary enjoyment, seems inevitable in any strongly developed sexual life, and is indisputably much safer, and more consonant with humanity and refinement, than the so-called safety-valve of prostitution. The black shadow of the Christian superstition has perpetuated needless ignorance and suffering here.

In short, sex is complex, and in humanity, largely mental and imaginative. Certain minor and occasional aberrations are part of the complete life. But the system of silence and repression, often reacts on women's organism in a thoroughly abnormal manner, and a completely *artificial* (this is the point) perversion may be established, and if it is established early enough, may be quite unconscious for years. And the more sensitive and diffident and amenable to ideas of modesty the girl is, the more easily may this process be developed.

Any direct external stimulation is much rarer among young girls than among boys of the same age and class. The actual physiology of women, as well as the sense of modesty and the fear of shocking and offending, will generally prevent this, either alone or with other girls, though here again there are many exceptions. But day-dreaming, the production of a high degree of excitement, and sometimes of the actual climax of enjoyment, by means of vague yet delightful imaginings, is the most exquisite pleasure and deepest secret of many imaginative and sensitive girls, and may even begin before puberty. The development of the heterosexual relation, either in marriage or with a lover, may supersede those experiences, and they remain a beautiful but temporary episode, or recur at intervals of loneliness between normal erotic activity. But in these days of suppressed desires and delayed marriages, it is more and more probable that the habit will become a necessity, and it may lead to a great difficulty in forming normal connections or even to an aversion thereto. I would even say that after twenty-five, the woman who has neither husband nor lover and is not under-vitalised and sexually deficient, is suffering mentally and bodily – often without knowing why she suffers; nervous irritated, anæmic, always tired, or ruthlessly and feverishly fussing over trifles; or else she has other consolations, which make her so-called 'chastity' a pernicious sham.

Artificial or substitute homosexuality – as distinct from true inversion – is very widely diffused among women, as a result of the repression of normal gratification and the segregation of the sexes, which still largely obtains. It appears, I think, later in life than onanism; in the later twenties or thirties rather than in the teens. Sometimes its only direct manifestations are quite noncommittal and platonic; but even this incomplete and timid homosexuality can always be distinguished from true affectionate friendship between women, by its jealous, exacting and extravagant tone. Of course, when one of the partners in such an attachment is a real or congenital invert, it is at once much more serious and much more physical. The psychology of homogenic women has been much less studied than that of inverted men. Probably there are many varieties and subtleties of emotional fibre among them. Some very great authorities have believed that the inverted woman is more often bisexual – less exclusively attracted to other women – than the inverted man. This view needs very careful confirmation, but if true, it would prove the greater plasticity of women's sex-impulse. It has also been stated that the invert, man or woman, is drawn towards the normal types of their own sex. These and other points, should be elucidated by the Society's work. Certainly, the heterosexual woman of passionate but shy and sensitive nature, is often responsive to the inverted woman's advances, especially if she is erotically ignorant and inexperienced. Also many women of quite normally directed (heterosexual) inclinations, realise in mature life, when they have experienced passion, that the devoted admiration and friendship they felt for certain girl friends, had a real, though perfectly unconscious, spark of desire in its exaltation and intensity; an unmistakable, indefinable note, which was absolutely lacking in many equally sincere and lasting friendships.

Neither artificial homosexuality nor prolonged auto-erotism – to use Havelock Ellis' masterly phrase – prove *innate* morbidity. Careful observation and many confidences from members of my own sex, have convinced me that our maintenance of outworn traditions is manufacturing habitual auto-erotists and perverts, out of women who would instinctively prefer the love of a man, who would bring them sympathy and comprehension as well as desire. I repudiate all wish to slight or depreciate the love-life of the real homosexual; but it cannot be advisable to force the growth of that habit in heterosexual people. And remember, there are other very dangerous and degrading perversions which may develop under repression. I know of a case in which a sudden, inexplicable, but apparently quite irresistible, lust of cruelty developed in a woman of the most actively kind and tender heart, but highly emotional and nervous, and sexually unsatisfied. As for the indirect psychic effects of involuntary and prolonged abstinence, surely Freud's researches can leave no doubt in the minds of thinking people. Here again, I know *personally* of a case of a fixed idea, which for three years developed recurrent spasms of maniacal terror.

Again, I ask, why all this waste of women, and of life?

The realities of women's sexual life have been greatly obscured by the lack of any sexual vocabulary. While her brother has often learned all the slang of the street before adolescence, the conventionally 'decently brought-up' girl, of the upper and middle classes, has no terms to define many of her sensations and experiences. When she marries, or meets her first lover, she learns a whole new language, and often this language has been defiled in the mind of the man who teaches it to her, long before they met.

There is one criticism which I want to forestall here. It will be said that, in women, the maternal instinct is inextricably interwoven with the sexual, and that, in ignoring this instinct, I have a very false perspective. I admit at once that a certain protective tenderness is part of any strong passion, or even amorous fancy, in nearly all women, though not the sole constituent. As to the love of one's own children, or the desire for children, I have tried to say nothing in this paper, that was not known to me, either through my own experience, or the observation and testimony of persons I know well. My conclusions are based on life, not on books, though I have been confirmed in my personal opinions and conclusions by some of the greatest psychologists, especially Dr Havelock Ellis, whose immense research is fused and illuminated by an inspired intuition.

I have no experience of maternity, nor of the desire for maternity, which is generally attributed to women. Also, I think much actual motherhood is unwilling, and this is an irremediable wrong to the Mother and the Child alike. Absolute freedom of choice on the woman's part, and intense desire both for her mate and her child, are the magic forces that will vitalise and transfigure the race. As it is, many women have no maternal longings at all, and they should never become mothers. If the Eugenics Education Society deserved its name, it would undertake in this country, the work that Margaret Sanger − to whom be honour and gratitude for ever! − is doing in America. In view of the gross neglect of women's interests as mothers and as citizens, and of the lean years before us all, the demand for a higher birthrate is both impudent and inhuman. The underhand opposition to the spread of contraceptive information must be overcome. The ineffably foolish laws penalising abortion must be abolished; they are one of the foulest remnants of the Canon Law. And if ecclesiastics and capitalists and militarists call for more births, let us remind them that a large percentage of young adult women are debarred from legal motherhood, and that, in spite of the War Baby Scoop, our Bastardy laws remain unaltered.

The eugenic aspect of sex and love has been very neatly summed up by a woman-poet, Anna Wickham:

> *The world whips frank, gay love with rods;*
> *But frankly, gaily, shall ye get the gods.*

F.W.STELLA BROWNE

UNIVERSITY OF GLAMORGAN
PRIFYSGOL MORGANNWG

Learning Resources
Centre

Appendix 2
'The Right to Abortion'
by F.W.Stella Browne
Introduced by Sheila Rowbotham

This is a shortened version of an article by Stella
Browne, 'The Right to Abortion' which appeared originally in
a book called *Abortion* in 1935. It was accompanied by two
other articles; one a plea for abortion on restricted grounds by
Dr Harry Roberts, who believed it should be available for
working-class women with real hardship but not for women
who had what he described as bohemian casual sexual relationships; the second was total opposition from A.M.Ludovici
was not only against abortion — he thought feminism was
masculinising women. Browne's article formed the basis of
her minority statement when ALRA gave evidence before
the Interdepartmental Committee on Abortion in 1937.

The sections which have been omitted relate to the
specific context in which Stella Browne was arguing for
abortion. She describes the hostile rulings of the churches and
the importance of the revolutionary example of the Soviet
Union in legalising abortion. In the 1920s and early 1930s
there were campaigns for legal abortion involving feminist
socialists and communists in Czechoslovakia, the Socialist
Republic of Vienna, Estonia, Denmark, Norway and France.
She also discussed the concern about maternal mortality in
Britain in the 1930s. The Labour Party insisted that
malnutrition and poverty were the only causes and they

refused to accept the evidence that a large proportion of cases were from abortion. She expressed the disillusionment which many women who had campaigned for birth control during the twenties must have felt about the imperviousness of the Labour Party, 'after years of feminist agitation and propaganda within its ranks', to issues which related to women's sexual lives. Working-class women's organisations were more sympathetic to abortion law reform than the Labour Party. Stella Browne quotes the important resolution passed by a majority of 1,340 to 20 at the Women's Co-op Guild Congress in Hartlepool in 1934. The resolution was moved by the Blackhorse branch and seconded by Elmers End. It was defended by Mme Lorsignol of West Chislehurst and Mrs Harvey of Holloway.

The resolution demanded, in view of the persistently high maternal death-rate and the evils arising from the illegal practice of abortion, that abortion should be made legal and carried out under the same conditions as any other surgical operation. The conference also wanted an amnesty for women in prison for abortion.

The campaign for birth control and the investigations of maternal mortality created pressure for abortion on restricted grounds. Stella Browne examines these arguments in detail and dismisses them as contradictory and impractical. She asserts a woman's right to choose or refuse maternity 'as an absolute right' but adds: 'up to the viability of the child'. It is not clear whether she thought there should be a time limit set upon the 'absolute right' to choose – though this would be uncharacteristic.

The question of the viability of the *foetus* has become a controversial issue in the present campaign for abortion. Campaigners are divided on whether abortion should be legal for up to only twenty-four or twenty-eight weeks or whether a woman should have the right to terminate a pregnancy at any point. There is though complete agreement with Stella Browne's concern that ideally abortion should be freely and easily available in the early stages of pregnancy.

The overwhelming force of Stella Browne's arguments for contraception and abortion are in terms of women's control over sexuality not as part of state population policy. She is careful to insist that no woman should be pressured into abortion by economic necessity. But she does refer to abortion for women of 'variant endocrine blend and psychological trend', a eugenic argument which has lurked behind some subsequent pressure for abortion. There is an important distinction between campaigning for abortion as part of the capitalist state's regulation of the poor and the arguments for sexual self-determination which have come from the women's liberation movement.

Stella Browne suggests in this article that abortion could be erotically preferable for some women given the forms of contraception which existed in the 1930s. Most women fighting for abortion now would see it as the necessary complement to contraception, not as an alternative, though it is true that the coil and menstrual extraction methods make the distinction between contraception and abortion less clear. Feminists in the modern women's movement share her dissatisfaction with the way in which research decisions are made about what to investigate or how to test new forms of contraception. One of the 'dragon's teeth' of imperialism, which she did not foresee, are experiments on women in developing countries. There is, too, a growing interest within the women's movement in the kind of folk remedies she describes. This need not mean that we dismiss all aspects of science but that we acknowledge we have still much to learn from less technological cultures.

The Right to Abortion
by F.W.Stella Browne

This essay aims at stating the case for freedom of choice by women as regards the continuation to term of pregnancy or its interruption by medical and scientific methods. It starts with the (as yet still rather unpopular) assumption that women are really human beings, and that freedom of choice and deliberate intention are necessary for them in their sexual relations and their maternity, if they are to make anything of their status and opportunities in certain communities today, and if they are to breed a race of greater powers and finer standards of value.

A DEFINITION

A definition of abortion is necessary, for many people are still apt to confuse this procedure with either contraceptive birth control or surgical sterilisation.

Abortion is the intentional termination of pregnancy. This may occur in the initial stages, when the female cell has fused with the spermatozoön and been fertilised, or when the conjoined cell has nested itself in the womb where it develops throughout the ten lunar months of gestation. Interruption of the later stages of gestation is a difficult and dangerous process, the dividing line being about the sixteenth week. The expulsion of the contents of the uterus, when occurring spontaneously or as a result of accident, is known as miscarriage. Abortion is not prevention of pregnancy during a given occasion of intercourse, i.e. contraception, nor removal of the capacity to conceive, i.e. sterilisation.

THE LAWS OF THE LAND

The legal view of abortion in this country is stated in the verbatim extract from a septuagenarian Statute prefixed to this book. Here, too, misunderstandings and delusions are prevalent. It cannot be too strongly stressed that the Statute of 1861 recognises NO exceptions: neither incest, nor rape, nor the communication of venereal disease, nor the abuse of mental defectives or of minor girls, nor extremes of poverty with no prospect of its future alleviation. The occasional exceptions whereby a merciful and modern-minded medical practitioner operates on a woman, under the protection of a written statement from one or two colleagues in his profession, certifying that in their opinion the operation is necessary to save the woman's life – these are wholly 'uncovenanted mercies'. They have grown up, like other things in our adaptable and empiric but incoherent social customs, as a concession which the law does not *officially* recognise. Under the influence of both feminist and humanitarian ideas, some of the younger generation of medical men and women will operate or give covering statements when the woman's health or reason are in jeopardy, not her life alone. But this, too, however significant of shifting values, is purely a concession, and it is neither just, nor dignified, nor intellectually honest that champions of women should accept such a concession and pin their hopes to its slow and piecemeal and extremely problematical extension without clarifying the issue and agitating for definite reform.

Moreover, in the world as it is at present, such 'hole-and-corner' rationality and humanity becomes inevitably *mainly* a privilege of the minority who can afford high fees and lengthy convalescence. That is to say, *what should be a normal and integral part of modern medicine and surgery is forced into the category of purchasable contraband,* and at once a vested interest is created in the breach of the law, while preserving its austere façade and the practice of widespread direct and indirect blackmail. It is hard to imagine any strictly limited and circumscribed reforms of the present law which would not be open to the same objection, and the narrower their scope the stronger the probability that the amended Law would be infringed . . .[1]

'MATERNAL MORTALITY' OR HUMAN SACRIFICE?

The maternal death-rate and its associated trail of disease and disability have spectacular force and wide appeal as arguments for the legalisation of abortion. They stir many sympathisers whom their logical implications and the entire case for freedom would – at least initially – alarm or repel. The same is true of those much rarer – but still not infrequent – and peculiarly pitiful cases where a young girl or a woman is made pregnant by rape or criminal assault, or through incest as the result of over-crowding or parental negligence or abuse. Such suffering is an indictment of the whole social system that tolerates its infliction and is the ultimate expression of the view of women as vessels – of 'honour' and 'dishonour' as the case may be – for men's use and as automatic breeding machines. But these cases do not include

[1] Cf. the words of the late Mr Justice McCardie, one of the greatest lawyers of our time: 'I pass over the cases of surgical practice of abortion, but I merely point to them to show that even they are publicly forbidden by the ludicrously wide terms of the Act.' Havelock Ellis in *Studies*, Vol. vi, traces the attitude of Classical Antiquity, the rise and formulation of Christian prohibitions, and the modern outlook.

the whole of the demand for women's right to abortion. That is based – as I see it – on justice rather than on pity; on the dignity of knowledge rather than the pathos of ignorance. And as these cases may be so emphasised as to exclude other circumstances and aspects from consideration, let us sift the peculiar danger of English opinion and English legislation – the Half-Way House, the tardy compromise inflicting injustice and indignity, but soothing 'public opinion' into the belief that something really helpful has been done.

AN ABSOLUTE RIGHT

The woman's right to abortion is an absolute right, as I see it, up to the viability of her child. It does not depend upon certainty of death for her if the child is carried to term, though such a certainty or probability is, of course, a double claim to this relief. It does not depend on damage or permanent injury to her physical or mental health, whether certain or probable, if her child is born at term. It does not depend on the number of her previous confinements: the suggestion, put forward by some vigorous and veteran agitators for abortion law reform, that the woman should first supply a quota of at least two children, seems to me to disregard the individual needs, nature, and conditions of women. Neither does the right to refuse an unwanted child depend on economic conditions, though these supply an almost universal argument in this era of unemployment. Neither does the right we claim depend on having obtained the sanction of the Law and the Church to live with some special man, to bear his name, and share his home and means. Abortion legal for married women only would be the final climax of the illogical absurdity of our respectability complex; but it is certain to be advocated in some quarters, and it is a perfect example of the narrowest Trade Union spirit. After all, is not contraception for married women only the slogan of much organised feminist respectability?

The right to abortion does not depend on crimes which the conventions of romantic tradition deem worse than death, and which laws justifiably treat as second only to murder. (It is an interesting question how far the reprobation of rape is a defence of women's dignity and personality and how far it is subconscious 'compensation', communal jealousy, and property defence.) These crimes are barbarous and tragic, but the victim, even the girl in her early teens, is legally compelled to carry and bring to birth the results of sexual violence, whose begetter is punished with the full rigour of the law. Cannot chivalry here be tempered with reason, justice, and common sense?

Neither does the right to abortion *depend* on the uncertain and unpredictable result of possible genetic patterns in the child. Heredity is a much more intricate problem than pre-Mendelian Darwinism supposed. Before birth, heredity – or at least *maternal* inheritance – and environment are hardly distinguishable, and the mother's food, habits, and mental and emotional reactions must have profound effects, through the metabolic rhythms which pass through her child's body from her own. Abortion must be the key to a new world for women, not a bulwark for things as they are, economically nor biologically. Abortion should not be either a perquisite of the legal wife only, nor merely a last remedy against illegitimacy. It should be available for any woman, without insolent inquisitions, nor ruinous financial charges, nor tangles of red tape. For our bodies are our own.

But what of the practical realisation of this principle? It seems to me that our case is as strong empirically as ethically, and that a severely circumscribed permission to terminate pregnancy would be attended by so many difficulties and cause so many injustices and absurdities that it would soon be found unworkable; just as the present law, for all its severity, is broken all over the country every day and by thousands of women, poor and rich, and by their helpers or exploiters, qualified or quacks.

MORE LIGHT

Let us examine possible *restricted concessions* of the right to termination of pregnancy; in every case, be it well understood, by means of qualified and skilled medical and surgical help. No supporter of the right to abortion wishes to hand women over to the clumsy, uncleanly, often futile and often fatal interferences of those who, in Mr George Bedborough's apt phrase, 'trade on the tragedy of despair', though there are cases of women who, whether with some midwifery training or a natural turn for practical medicine, have come to the aid of their friends and neighbours in this way, almost habitually, and earned thanks and blessings instead of bringing disaster. Nevertheless the attendant risks, without exact knowledge of the patient's circumstances and peculiarities and general constitution, and without the fullest opportunities for antiseptic and aseptic precautions, are too great. They need never occur under a law which honestly faced and humanely provided for the need to avert unwanted motherhood.

The mere fact that operations could be performed thoroughly and need not be scrambled through with eyes and ears alert for possible interruptions would save thousands of lives. So would the mercy of the *right* to a few days' rest in bed, with cleanliness and quiet, drowsing and light food; without inquiries and subterfuges, feverish fears, and those dread sudden chills. The trail of disease and crippling injuries, displacements, discharges, hæmorrhages, inflammations, after unskilled – or even skilled but subsequently neglected – 'illegal operations' is as much a human sacrifice as the more spectacular death-roll itself.

An adequate abortion law would also encourage *constructive* research. There is no reason to suppose that we are at more than the mere alphabet of chemistry and psycho-biology in this matter. It is true that nearly all the vegetable potions used in traditional and current folk-lore to procure abortion are only effective in dosages which may inflict permanent injury, especially on heart, kidneys, and organs of elimination. But individual differences – 'idiosyncrasies' – here are very great. Throughout the islands of the Pacific, and in Mexico and Central America as well as Indonesia, there is a highly skilled and carefully guarded technique which attains results without slaughtering or crippling women. Missionaries have failed to extirpate this accomplishment, and anthro-pologists have testified to its admirable efficacy. Is it perhaps – together with the whole erotic art of the islands – a heritage from the Areoi or from a past far more remote? In any case, the invention and circulation of a perfectly reliable and otherwise tolerable abortifacient – especially if it could be self-administered, either by the mouth or as injections, intravenous or intra-muscular – would be the greatest gift science could give to women. This triumph is perhaps possible within measurable time – unless indeed such civilisation as Europe has achieved should pass away under a deluge of the high explosives and poison gases which afford so lucrative and respectable a branch of research and industry. The right to abortion is a key-point, going deep down to the roots of social philosophy and economic reality . . .

LIMITATION IS STULTIFICATION

The right to abortion should be taken quite away from

legal technicality and legal controversy. Up to the viability of her child, it is as much a woman's right as the removal of a dangerously diseased appendix. It is more difficult and more fraught with danger in the middle months of pregnancy than in its early weeks. Therefore it should be made available safely and cleanly and as promptly as possible to all who require it. Though, in view of the extreme emotional instability of pregnancy, and the frequent and violent changes of mood in many women when with child, it would be wise to give any woman demanding abortion – unless in the gravest circumstances – a fortnight or three weeks in which to think over her decision. But this time for reflection should never become an excuse for refusal to operate, if the woman sticks to her guns and repeats her wish.

CONTRACEPTION AS CONVENTION

The present writer will hardly be accused of lukewarmness or hostility to birth control by the methods legally permitted since the great fight of Charles Bradlaugh and Annie Besant in 1877. But of recent years the cant of continence has been supplemented by what is rather like cant about contraception. No contraceptive at present accessible to the public is 100 per cent reliable, and at the same time cheap, easy to store and to apply, otherwise non-injurious and æsthetically satisfactory. Moreover, there is almost incredible profiteering in the sale of these articles, and the housing[1] of the majority of our people with its overcrowding and lack of constant hot-water supply is an incessant hindrance to contraception *in actual practice*. Also, there is extreme individual diversity between one person and another in sexual matters, organically, functionally, and in psychic

[1] Cf. the sympathetic and realistic study *Birth Control on Trial*, by Mrs Lella Secor Florence (London; George Allen & Unwin Ltd).

and emotional attitudes. Methods which work admirably between one couple of partners may and do fail dismally or disastrously with another, or may be successful for some time and then fail or become impracticable. This is perfectly well known to all serious students or teachers of birth control. *Why, then*, should abortion not be freely available for all, if and when contraceptives fail? The knowledge that a sure second line of defence was available without subterfuge or extortion, should contraception fail, would save the racked nerves of thousands of sensitive women and men, and prevent the shipwreck of much mutual joy and affection. If once the control of reproduction is accepted – and it is as much a part of our heritage and our achievement as the use of fire, articulate speech, agriculture, mechanical transport, sanitation, etc. – the exact method becomes a matter of individual preference and/or expediency, whether by contraception, coital technique, abortion, or voluntary sterilisation.

But the psychological difficulties of low-grade intelligence in poverty are great, and in the flight from freedom I know of no more curious suggestion than that abortion should be legally available only for women who have not neglected to use contraceptives, or who have not been careless of instructions duly imparted. Of course, much human mentality is of a very poor quality and not improved by the material conditions in which it struggles to live – or simply vegetates. Also, for generations women have been discouraged in any independent thought or action in sexual matters; they have been systematically stultified, kept ignorant and dependent. Granted; but why punish them by insisting on unwanted births? Humanity is fallible and we have all committed follies and stupidities of various kinds, without incurring anything like such condign punishment. What of the child carried to term as a definite punishment?

Who is to assess or collect the fines which have been suggested as appropriate in such cases? *How is the negligence to be proved?* Is it to be thought tolerable that the man should denounce his partner? Is the woman to be cross-examined on the most intimate physical details? *Or are we to install a dictaphone in every room; a moralist under every bed?*

'MORE BRAIN, O LORD!'

Of course, all this is an additional argument for intelligence, knowledge, responsibility, civilisation: 'More Brain, O Lord!' Especially an argument for a wider variety and greater security in contraceptives, and for a public policy which makes such contraceptives available at possible prices. It is also an argument for accuracy, sympathy, and candour in the study and treatment of sex, especially of the sexual sentiments and needs of women, and also for adequate housing, for economic justice, for international peace: stretching out from the bodies and beds of human lovers to all the dangers and dreams, hopes and achievements of the world today and the conquest of the future.

In that future, if it should be dominated by the human brain and will, and 'moulded nearer to the heart's desire', children will be welcomed and created as achievements, and not flung into life with fear and anger as disastrous accidents. In present circumstances there is no doubt that many women procure miscarriages intentionally, for economic reasons, when, left to their own choice, they would prefer to have the children. In the world we are trying to build, the maternal woman will not be sterilised, and the woman of variant endocrine blend and psychological trend will not be obliged to have nervously unbalanced and devitalised children whom she neither wants nor understands.

Constructive civilisation *would not only restrict but also release heredity.* It would not sacrifice the possibilities of genetic variety and superiority to a marriage system whose bankruptcy is patent to all. In the words of a pioneering reformer who has championed many unpopular minorities and many neglected truths: 'When we sweep away the superstitious cobwebs which prevent healthy women from having children they desire by men whom they desire, the destiny of man will take excellent care of itself.'[1] I would also cite the recorded view of two devoted and successful medical sociologists, Drs Innes Pearse and Williamson, in *The Case for Action*. They say, 'The sense of responsibility of mothers, at any rate, towards the children they bear is increasing. This explains the fact that the urgency of the desire to terminate as well as to avoid pregnancies is growing.' Yes, some maternal women are abortionists of necessity, and with resentment and regret. Their problem will be solved if a constructive civilisation should be built up. It is being met today in Soviet Russia. But there are women who are not primarily maternal, who love their own vanity or their own dreams, or some creative call of work; or a man, or more than one man, or another woman, more than any child. These women exist. Their exact percentage may be small – I do not think it is – but their total number is large.

MASCULINE MYTHOLOGY

The justifiability and indeed the very existence of such individualities and such variant types has been hotly

[1] R.B.Kerr in the *New Generation*, May 1932. Cf. also Alec Craig in *Sex and Revolution*, p.100 (George Allen & Unwin Ltd). 'The marriage law of this country is rapidly becoming unworkable. It is becoming absurd, not only to a few intellectuals, but in the eyes of the ordinary man. It has lost its moral hold, not only in Bloomsbury and Mayfair, but in Tooting and Manchester.'

contested, not only by traditional sentimentalists but by healers and *savants* to whom, in many ways, we owe much. But they deduce the whole woman from her uterus only! and when women themselves protest, however moderately, against all being cut to pattern, the response of the mythologists has often contained more hot air than illumination. Under the inhuman ideals of the patriarchate and the ascetic traditions of Christianity, even love between husband and wife was suspect, except as a prelude to parenthood. Acton, one of the leaders of British medicine in the early nineteenth century, wrote that to attribute sexual feelings to women was a 'vile aspersion' and termed women 'lascivious' if they experienced sexual desire 'even in the embrace of their husbands'.

THE EROTIC ASPECT OF ABORTION

Well, the most enlightened circles in this country and America have got a little farther than that; the work of such authorities as Van de Velde, Dickinson, G.V.Hamilton, Katharine Bement Davis, is supplementing and supporting the pioneer studies of Havelock Ellis. The economic independence of many women – partial and precarious as it is! – has done more service to truth than centuries of subjection and subterfuge under Christian auspices. But old fetters clog even when they have fallen, and many women are still afraid to say that for them abortion is not only ethically permissible and practically necessary but also erotically preferable to any current and available form of contraception, because any available contraceptive disturbs the essential rhythm, the crescendo, climax, and diminuendo of the communion of sex.

Here the essential factor is the variety of structure, of chemical constitution, of psychic associations and reactions in regard to sex: the most intimate and individual of all organic phases and functions, and yet the one in which our traditions and conventions allow least scope for diversity. And this ironclad ignorance is made worse by the still prevalent lack of erotic knowledge and skill. Western Europe and America have brought much knowledge, much expansion – even very painful expansion – of experience to the coloured races and the Ancient East: some of their gifts have been dragons' teeth, and of that harvest we have not yet seen the end. But they have also brought good things and among them modern sanitary and contraceptive service. And in return for the science of health and birth we are beginning to realise, and perhaps also here and there to acquire, something of the Asiatic and Pacific peoples' art of love.

Undoubtedly there are many women today in whom the wish for a child would grow out of complete sensation and gratification, *were they once achieved*. There are others for whom that 'flame flower' would be its own sanction and its own fruit. Why not? There are many ways of love and many grades and phases.

The individual differences are endless. But there are many women, and perhaps women whose desire for their partners, whose awareness of their partner's personality is specially ardent and acute, who require either deep penetration or impregnation for their full expression. *But they do not want children*; or at least not all the children they would otherwise conceive. Their prescription is obvious: safe, honest, expert termination of pregnancy at their demand. And only a tradition that has manufactured and still manufactures both mental and sexual cripples could dispute this remedy.

Two points could be mentioned, one comparatively trivial and local, the other basic.

THE RIGHTS OF THE HUSBAND

In my opinion, any woman, whether married or not, should be able to refuse maternity even after conception. But if the husband of a married woman particularly desires children, and she persistently refuses, he should be able to obtain a divorce on the ground of her refusal, and to seek fatherhood and happiness with some other woman. The divorce should be a quick, cheap, and decent procedure, not the excruciating exposure and ruinous expense of today. But the crying need for divorce reform and marriage reform is another story.

THE SIFTING OF SOULS

Finally, I deny that the right to abortion utterly contravenes any belief in either the possibility of human survival or the mystery of human consciousness and human personality. It seems to me that those who support the case for reincarnation or continuation must regard human parental responsibility as an important factor in the sifting of souls, and for really effective responsibility, abortion is as necessary an instrument as contraception. This view will not commend itself to some of our keenest fighters, but it seems to me worth the consideration of those who take the theosophical − or other angles of the mystical − view of human destiny and cosmic forces.

The modern outlook does not apologise for, nor whine about, sex. Nor does it see the whole purpose of sex as begun and ended in parenthood. If sexual experience for the modern person has been fused and illuminated by the overwhelming vision and emotion of love, sex will be inestimably precious and significant, whether or not the fruit of life should result. Even apart from love or deep affection or imaginative inspiration – none of which can be had to order! – even at its most experimental and casual, sex for moderns will have its use and value apart from parenthood. Indeed, our modern consciences are apt to shrink from linking children to casual and impersonal sex contacts, though we may experience these with pleasure and honest appreciation.

But parenthood is a responsibility or, if you will, a privilege for the sanest, finest, and most vital yet altruistic. And in making children for the world, let them not forget that the world needs re-making for the children.

*   *   *

'No considerations justify the enforcement of child-bearing.'
Memorandum of the Federation of Progressive Societies and Individuals on Sexual Law and Convention, January 1935.

The world whips frank, gay love with rods;
But frankly, gaily, shall ye get the gods.

ANNA WICKHAM

Index